Potato Pals 2

# User's Guide

## PATRICK JACKSON • RIE KIMURA

OXFORD
UNIVERSITY PRESS

# OXFORD
## UNIVERSITY PRESS

198 Madison Avenue
New York, NY 10016 USA

Great Clarendon Street, Oxford OX2 6DP UK

Oxford University Press is a department of the University of Oxford.
It furthers the University's objective of excellence in research, scholarship,
and education by publishing worldwide in

Oxford  New York

Auckland  Cape Town  Dar es Salaam  Hong Kong  Karachi
Kuala Lumpur  Madrid  Melbourne  Mexico City  Nairobi
New Delhi  Shanghai  Taipei  Toronto

With offices in

Argentina  Austria  Brazil  Chile  Czech Republic  France  Greece
Guatemala  Hungary  Italy  Japan  Poland  Portugal  Singapore
South Korea  Switzerland  Thailand  Turkey  Ukraine  Vietnam

OXFORD and OXFORD ENGLISH are registered trademarks of
Oxford University Press

© Oxford University Press 2005

ISBN-13: 978 0 19 439197 9
ISBN-10: 0 19 439197 3

Editorial Manager: Nancy Leonhardt
Senior Editor: Paul Phillips
Editor: Joseph McGasko
Art Director: Maj-Britt Hagsted
Senior Designer: Mia Gomez
Production Manager: Shanta Persaud
Production Controller: Eve Wong

Illustrations by Rie Kimura

Additional realia by Mia Gomez

Printing (last digit): 10 9 8 7 6 5 4 3 2 1

Printed in Hong Kong.

### Acknowledgements:

Thanks to all the people who have made this dream come true:
Naomi Sogabe, Yoko Hinoshita, and the teachers at the Potato Club, where it all began.

Chris Bond, Mayuka Habbick, Robert Habbick, Alexandra Jackson-Kay, Robert Faber,
Amanda Park, Neil Blair, William Lacy, Deborah Sanderson, Paul Riley, Naoko Ogikubo,
Jane Blackstock, and Peter Warner for practical help and encouragement.

Our wonderful editors and designers at Oxford University Press.

P.J. and R.K.


For Ami and Kai, who have been surrounded by potatoes since they were born,
and my darling Yuko, whom I love so much. P.J.
For Yoshimasa Kimura, who supported me in every respect. R.K.

# What's Inside the User's Guide?

WELCOME!

Welcome to the **Potato Pals 2 User's Guide**! In this book you will learn all about the **Potato Pals** series of books: what they are, why they are useful, and how you and your students can get the most out of them. We hope that along the way you discover many helpful hints and new ideas for teaching students to speak, read, and enjoy English.

## What is *Potato Pals*?

**Potato Pals** is a program for learning English through reading that gives students a new way of developing language skills. Using a unique system of picture cues, **Potato Pals** helps students to remember useful language and use it over and over. **Potato Pals** also teaches new vocabulary words and topics that relate to this language. Best of all, **Potato Pals** features the Potato Pals themselves, six friendly spuds your students will love!

## Why use *Potato Pals*?

Children love to talk about themselves. They also love to play! **Potato Pals** is a program for learning English that gives students the words to talk about their daily lives. It shows many different ways to use these words, and it has a lot of fun games and activities. Students learn useful, everyday English while having fun!

That's the Potato Pals way!

## Who should use *Potato Pals*?

**Potato Pals** is for any teacher who wants to teach English in an active, fun way. Students can start to use English immediately. They feel good about themselves and want to learn more!

**Potato Pals** is also a great resource for parents who want to teach their children at home. Parents can help their children learn while they enjoy reading and playing together!

We want students, teachers, and parents to have fun while teaching and learning. We think that **Potato Pals** can make this happen!

# What does *Potato Pals* include?

**Potato Pals 2** has four main parts in its program:

**1**   **The Book Set: Six Books and a CD**

 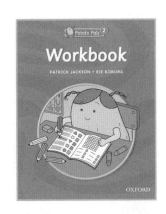

**2**   **The Practice Books: Activity Book and Workbook**

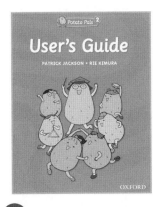 

**3**   **The User's Guide**     **4**   **The Picture Cards**

You can use some or all of these parts to make **Potato Pals** work for you!

# Overview of Potato Pals Materials
# The Book Set Readers

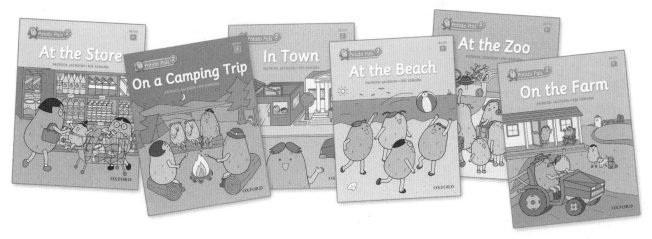

The readers are at the heart of the **Potato Pals** course. Story time is the favorite part of the lesson for many students. We want to help you make story time great every time. Follow the Potato Pals as they go out and about with their families. You will have fun, and so will your students!

## How do I use the readers?

Each book has a simple story. The story of each book introduces students to eight sentences. Students can learn these sentences and immediately use them to describe their daily lives.

Each book uses a special system called **Memoricons**. Memoricons are the small pictures that appear on every other page as you read the book. The Memoricons give students the chance to review as they read. They will love the challenge of remembering:

• What the icon represents

• How to say it in English!

Here's how it works:

**Each left-hand page has a stem phrase. This is also the title of the book. It tells you where the story takes place or what the theme is. Chanting, singing, and miming this phrase is one way to have fun while learning it.**

**Each right-hand page has the rest of the sentence. This sentence is illustrated by a large picture above it.**

Together, the stem phrase and the sentence are called the Story Sentence. After you go over it a few times, students can read the Story Sentence "At the beach, we put on sun block."

**When you turn the page, the stem phrase is still there on the left-hand page. But now there is also a Memoricon. This is a picture cue that reminds students about the previous page.**

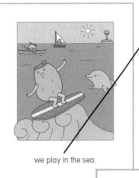

**At the same time, a new sentence is introduced on the right-hand page.**

**Students can now read two Story Sentences: "At the beach, we put on sunblock. We play in the sea."**

Now when you turn the page, there are two Memoricons. They remind students about the two previous Story Sentences. Each new sentence builds on the sentence before it, so students feel confident about learning—and using—the new words!

With every new page, a new sentence is added. By the time students finish the last page, they should be able to read the book just by looking at the eight Memoricons. Then, they can talk about their own lives using the same words!

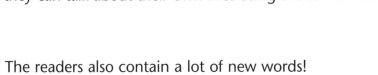

The readers also contain a lot of new words! There are two kinds of words in **Potato Pals**:

**1.** Focus Words

**2.** Topic Words

Focus Words are the names for common objects that can be found in the scenes. Each **Potato Pals** book has a group of Focus Words. You can teach these words as you read the book.

Each reader also has a group of Topic Words. These are words with a common theme, such as vehicles, adjectives, or telling the time. Each Topic Word is put in a natural context so students can remember it easily.

*That's great!*

In "At the Beach," the Topic Words are adjectives. Each picture features one adjective. On this page, the featured adjective is "empty." By the end of the book, students will know eight adjectives!

The Topic Words also make it easy to teach Question and Answer patterns. There is a Q & A pattern for each set of Topic Words. For example, for "At the Beach," you can ask *What's the picnic basket like?* Students answer *It's empty!* These patterns are included in this **User's Guide**.

As you can see, there are a lot of different things to teach in **Potato Pals** if you know where to look! This **User's Guide** will help you get the most out of every book.

# What are the stories in the readers?

Dean, his little sister Dee, and Mom are doing the shopping.

Daisy goes camping in the forest with Mom and Dad and her twin sisters.

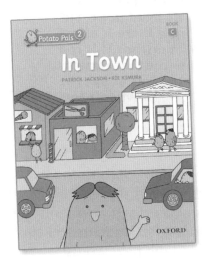

Chip and his friends show us a lot of things to see and do around Potatotown!

It's a beautiful day with Nina and her family by the sea.

Buddy loves to go to the zoo. So does his little brother Buzz!

What fun when Joy visits her grandparents' farm!

## What are the topics of the readers?

 **At the Store**: Action verbs

 **On a Camping Trip**: Adjectives

 **In Town**: Vehicles

 **At the Beach**: More adjectives

 **At the Zoo**: Telling the time

 **On the Farm**: Family members

## How will the User's Guide help me use the readers?

The **User's Guide** contains the following helpful features:

- "At a Glance" pages tell you right away what the Story Sentences, Focus Words, and Topic Words are for each book.
- Each book is separated into four lessons that you can teach in book order or in your own order.
- Games and activities support the language that is being learned.
- Sample presentations at the back of the book give you ideas about how to present the books (see page 85).

# The CD

## What is the CD?

The books come to life! The CD is part of the Book Set. It can be used in the classroom or listened to while looking at the stories at home. Your students will learn more quickly by doing both. This gives teachers and parents an answer to the question, "What can I do at home to help my students learn faster?" The CD contains:

**Focused**

**Readings**

**Point and Say**

**Activities**

**Fun**

**Songs**

**Three** readings of each book are included on the CD. The **first** reading is a simple reading of the book. The **second** reading includes sound effects that help students remember the sentences. The **third** reading includes Point and Say Activities. Every book also includes a catchy song, and there is a Potato Pals Theme Song that you can sing before every lesson! (See page 77 for the lyrics to this song.)

We like to say that Potato Pals readers are "books you can sing"! You can point to the Memoricons and mime the sentences as you sing the songs, either showing the students the last page of the reader, or by using the Picture Cards (see page 12). Students will learn proper pronunciation, enjoy themselves, and remember the sentences naturally while connecting the language with the actions and the music.

## How will the User's Guide help me with the CD?

The **User's Guide** contains the following helpful features:

- Full song lyrics on every "At a Glance" page.
- Easy-to-find track references.
- Suggestions in each lesson about when you should listen to the CD.
- A listing of all the Point and Say words from the Readings (see page 82).

**Use the CD in school and at home for the best results!**

# The Practice Books

**Potato Pals 2** includes two practice books: the **Activity Book** and the **Workbook**. These books give students more practice with the Story Sentences, Focus Words, Topic Words, and some of the phonics sounds from all six readers in the series. Each book has one unit in the practice books. These books were designed to be used either in the classroom or at home.

## What should I know about the practice books?

The **Activity Book** is for students who are just starting to learn English. The activities in this book will develop their cognitive skills, pencil control, and passive recognition of letters and printed words. They do not need to know any English to enjoy this book.

The **Workbook** is for students who know some English and can remember or refer to the language in the readers. Students will write simple words but not whole sentences. Students will need more teacher guidance with the **Workbook** than with the **Activity Book**.

Both books feature a space at the bottom of each page for teachers or parents to check and sign their children's work. This makes following a student's progress much easier!

## How do I use the practice books?

Make sure students take their time with each page. It is important, especially for very young learners, to say the words on the page wherever possible. It is much better to do one or two pages thoroughly than to rush through a large number of pages. The User's Guide suggests when to do certain pages.

Let's take a look at the first unit in the **Activity Book**. This is the unit that reviews the reader "At the Store." The other units all follow the same pattern. The **Workbook** also follows this structure.

## The Story Pages

These two pages practice the eight Story Sentences from the reader.

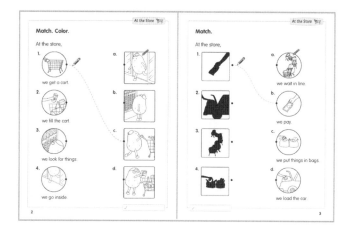

## The Vocabulary Pages

These two pages practice the Focus Words.

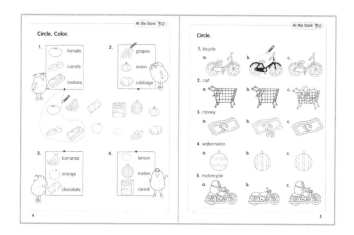

## The Topic Pages

The topic of "At the Store" is action verbs and these two pages have verb-related activities. Students practice the Topic Words.

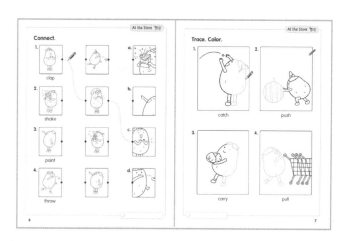

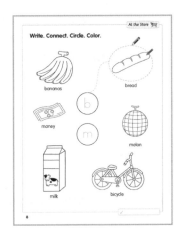

### The Phonics Page

This is the final page in the unit. It gives students additional vocabulary and phonics practice.

You will find an answer key and instructions for each page in the **Activity Book** and the **Workbook** on pages 89–92 of this **User's Guide**.

# The Picture Cards

**Potato Pals 2 Picture Cards** contain all of the Story Sentences, Focus Words, and Topic Words from the Book Set. The **Picture Cards** can be very useful for teaching the sentences and new words in **Potato Pals**. The **Picture Cards** can be used as:

- Flashcards to present the sentences and words during readings or songs.
- Game cards to reinforce learning.
- Cards to build giant card houses!

The cards are the perfect size for you to show in class, but they are also a good size for the small hands of your students!

Many of the activities in this **User's Guide** use the **Picture Cards**, so it will help you to get them if you can. If you can't, try to make your own. Picture cards are a great way to teach new words.

# The Lessons

The biggest section in this **User's Guide** are the lesson plans. They will help you use **Potato Pals** in the way that works best for you.

## How are the lessons organized?

Each unit of the **User's Guide** (A–F) covers one book. The unit starts with an "At a Glance" chart that shows you the language from the book, the lyrics for the song, what **Picture Cards** you need, and what tracks on the CD to use. This page gives you a quick overview of what you need to cover.

After the "At a Glance" page, the teaching of each book is divided into four lessons. The first lesson concentrates on the Story Sentences, the second teaches the Focus Words, the third covers the Topic Words, and the fourth is a complete review.

Story Sentences ⟷ Focus Words ⟷ Topic Words ⟷ Review

Each lesson includes:

• A prediction activity which will help students focus on the task ahead.

• A reading that focuses on a different aspect of the book.

• Two practice activities. You can choose one or use both.

• Three games suitable for reinforcing the target language.

• Information needed to do the relevant practice book pages.

## How long is each lesson?

Depending on how much time you have available, we suggest you mix and match to suit your students' needs. Here are some examples of what you can do for certain amounts of time:

| 5-minute lesson | reading, song |
| --- | --- |
| 10-minute lesson | reading, song, one activity or game |
| 20-minute lesson | prediction phase, reading, song, one activity, one game |
| 40-minute lesson | practice book check, prediction phase, reading, song, one or two activities, a game, an activity to end the class |

The lesson plans are very flexible, so you can put together the right combination for your students!

## When should I use *Potato Pals*?

We encourage you to pick, choose, and adapt. You know what suits your students best. You can:

• Fill an entire lesson by using all the activities suggested in this guide.

• Make **Potato Pals** the core of the lesson and add materials from other sources.

• Use **Potato Pals** to supplement a lesson in which you are covering the story, one of the topics, or some of the vocabulary from the readers.

• Reach for **Potato Pals** when you have a few minutes to spare, to refresh or reward a "tired" class.

# Potato Tips!

The **Potato Pals User's Guide** will help teachers in the classroom and parents who are teaching their kids at home. There are many methods of teaching, but here is some tried and true advice!

## Plan

The better you can plan your lessons, the better they will be. Visualize each step of the lesson and try to predict how long each step will take.

## Prepare

- Make sure everyone is prepared to learn by bringing the correct materials.
- Encourage everyone to do homework and praise them when they have done it.
- Set clear goals that students can achieve.
- Make a path to reach those goals.

## Pace

Some classes need a faster pace and some need a slower pace. Make sure your students are comfortable with the pace of the lesson.

## Play

Your lessons should be playful! Young students respond best and learn most if they feel that they are at play. There are many games in this book. You will know some of them and some will be new to you. Use them and enjoy them!

## Physical Response

Get your students moving around the room. No student likes to stay in one place for too long. This is also the fastest way for them to learn. There is a lot of miming, gesturing, and dancing included in **Potato Pals**. Get moving!

## Projects

You will find some photocopiable ideas for craft mini-projects in this book. These projects can be done in the classroom or as homework. Show and tell!

## Personalize

Real communication will help students develop real confidence. Remember to:

- Give students a chance to talk about themselves.
- Tell them about yourself.
- Encourage them to use the language at home.

This guide contains a few fresh ideas as to how to do this as well as some old favorites.

## Positive Energy

Believe in yourself and believe in your students. Be filled with positive energy! It really works!

## Prediction

This gives students a chance to share what they already know. Focus them on the learning about to take place. The ability to predict what's ahead is important when learning a new language. It's also really fun when you're right!

## Praise

Praise your students! Always tell them when they have done well. Everyone likes to be told they're great!

By making sure you follow these Potato Pal "P" words, you will have a very successful and happy bunch of potatoes!

# The Games

**Potato Pals 2 User's Guide** includes many different games that you can use to practice the language from the readers. All of these games are very language-focused, but some also practice other skills, including physical skills such as tossing a bean bag or jumping. We think it's important that students get up and move! Nothing makes language-learning easier than using the whole body to learn. We hope that you and your students enjoy playing these games.

Certain games are used more than once in this book. These games are our favorites! We feel that they are some of the most useful ones for teaching the language. We have provided three different choices for each lesson. If you do not have time to do all of the games, you can pick the one that you like best. You can also use many of the games in other lessons where they do not appear. The games are very flexible, and if you have a favorite, please use it whenever you feel it works best!

Each game in this book shows the following information:

**The ideal number of students who can play the game comfortably**

**The skills practiced by the game**

**The appropriate student age range for the game**

## Potato Games

### Game 1: Potato Grab

**Players:** 2–8
**Skills:** Vocabulary
**Age:** 3 and up

**Home use:** Yes
**Time:** 5–15 minutes
**You need:** Picture cards 44–65

**Where the game can be used, in a classroom or at home**

**How long the game will take**

**What materials you need to play the game**

This information can be used to help you plan your lesson and decide which game is best for you.

Try to have students use English as often as possible when they are playing the games. Teach some of these sentences to your students so that they can use them during games:

- *It's your turn.*
- *It's my turn.*
- *Well done!*
- *You're lucky!*
- *I don't know.*
- *That's hard.*
- *That's easy.*
- *Help me, please.*
- *Take a card.*
- *Roll the die.*

Make sure to have students count in English while playing board games and other games involving numbers.

One final note on competition: Many of the games in this **User's Guide** are not competitive games, but they can be made competitive if you want them to be. While competitive games can be good motivators, it is not fun for someone to lose all of the time! Try to avoid playing games that always use the same skills, and try to take different approaches to the same games. This will prevent the same students from always winning. You can also pair students of different ability, or give "head starts" to students who need more time. Make sure everyone has a chance to have a moment of potato glory!

# Points to Remember!

Sometimes practical points are very important to remember when you are teaching something new. Below are some practical suggestions that you can remember as you teach **Potato Pals** in class or at home.

- Talk as much in English as you can. Even if students can't understand everything you are saying, listening to you will still help them get used to the sound of English.

- People learn in different ways. Varying your presentation will keep you and your students happy.

- Language is sound. Children love to play with all sorts of sounds by whispering, shouting, and making funny noises. Chant the language while using objects and instruments to make sounds.

- Decorate the classroom with posters and other visual material. Labeling objects will help children learn to read.

- Start and finish elements of the lesson with something fun. This will give students structures that they can learn and look forward to every time you meet. We have provided the "Potato Pals Theme Song" as an example of something fun you can do in each class that will warm up the students—and you!

- Make a classroom bulletin board and cover it with students' pictures, news, letters, and photos.

- Keep your classroom tidy and organized. Regularly sort out your materials. It's a great way to get new ideas and remind yourself of old gems.

- Sticker charts are a super way to motivate children. Have a special treat or play a favorite game when they get to the goal.

- It's better to stop a game or activity while it's still fresh than to play it until students start to get bored. This way, students will look forward to playing the game again.

- Regular practice in small amounts will produce much better results than very long sessions.

- Part of every lesson should be review of what you studied in the previous lessons. Language ability is like all other skills—if you don't use it, you lose it!

# At a Glance

## Book A: At the Store

### Story Sentences

At the store, we get a cart.

At the store, we go inside.

At the store, we look for things.

At the store, we fill the cart.

At the store, we wait in line.

At the store, we pay.

At the store, we put things in bags.

At the store, we load the car.

### Focus Words

| | |
|---|---|
| 1. bicycle | 11. cereal |
| 2. cart | 12. tomato |
| 3. onion | 13. cookies |
| 4. carrots | 14. melon |
| 5. cabbage | 15. money |
| 6. bananas | 16. cheese |
| 7. orange | 17. chocolate |
| 8. grapes | 18. lemon |
| 9. bread | 19. watermelon |
| 10. milk | 20. motorcycle |

### Topic Words

Action verbs:

| | |
|---|---|
| 1. pull | 5. throw |
| 2. push | 6. catch |
| 3. point | 7. clap |
| 4. shake | 8. carry |

### Lyrics

**"At the Store"**

*Chorus:*

At the store
At the store
At the store, at the store
At the store, we get a cart
At the store, at the store
At the store, we go inside

At the store, at the store
At the store, we look for things
At the store, at the store
At the store, we fill the cart

*Chorus*

At the store, at the store
At the store, we wait in line
At the store, at the store
At the store, we pay

At the store, at the store
At the store, we put things in bags
At the store, at the store
At the store, we load the car

*Chorus*

### Picture Cards

Use Picture Cards 1–8 (Story Sentences), 9–28 (Focus Words), and 29–36 (Topic Words).

### CD

Track numbers 3–16 (song is on Track 16)

# Story Sentences

At the store, we get a cart.
At the store, we go inside.
At the store, we look for things.
At the store, we fill the cart.
At the store, we wait in line.
At the store, we pay.
At the store, we put things in bags.
At the store, we load the car.

1. We get a cart. (Pretend to be pushing and pulling a shopping cart.)

2. We go inside. (Make your arms into automatic doors that open in front of you as you "go inside.")

3. We look for things. (Put your fingers on your chin and look really puzzled.)

4. We fill the cart. (Pretend to be putting a lot of things into a cart.)

5. We wait in line. (Cross your arms and look from side to side. Pretend that you have been waiting for a long time.)

6. We pay. (Take out a purse or wallet and mime paying a clerk.)

7. We put things in bags. (Pretend to fill some shopping bags.)

8. We load the car. (Pretend to open the trunk of a car and put in some heavy objects.)

Now ask individual students to mime the sentences and have the other students say what they are doing.

##  Potato Story Time

### Prediction

Look at the cover of "At the Store" with the students. Focus them on the idea of shopping. Ask them where they go shopping, who they go with, and what they like to buy. Explain that "At the Store" is a book about Dean, his mom, and his little sister Dee going grocery shopping.

### Reading

Read "At the Store" or play Tracks 3 and 4 of the CD. Use the Memoricons (see page 6) and have your students repeat as many of the sentences or parts of the sentences as they can.

**NOTE:** Do not expect too much from this first reading. Your students will probably only be able to repeat bits and pieces. Praise their efforts!

## Potato Activities

### Activity 1

Show the eight Story Sentence picture cards one at a time. Mime the sentences for your students and then do them together:

### Activity 2

All the students make a circle. Pass the student on your left the card for *We get a cart* and say the sentence. The student passes the card to the next student to the left and repeats the sentence. Add more cards to the circle and have students pass them around faster and faster!

**OPTION:** Replace the cards with the mimed movements for the phrases.

##  Potato Song Time

Play Track 16 on the CD and sing the song with the students while doing the movements. Display the Story Sentence picture cards so that the students can see them clearly. Sing the song again while pointing at the cards. As an option, students can take turns singing different lines of the song.

## Potato Games

### Game 1: Potato Roll

**Players:** 2–20
**Skills:** Story Sentences, counting
**Age:** 4 and up
**Home use:** Yes
**Time:** 10–15 minutes
**You need:** 2 large homemade dice

Make a die out of recycled materials. You can use milk cartons or something similar. The die should be big enough for all the students to see when it is rolled. Decorate each side of the die with a Story Sentence Memoricon. Students take turns rolling the die and saying the sentences that come up. They get one point for each sentence they can say correctly. Keep score on the board and play to a time limit or up to a certain number of points. This game can be played as a team game.

**OPTION:** Add a number to each side of the die so that students get different amounts of points for different Story Sentences they can say. Use higher numbers for the sentences that are harder to say.

### Game 2: Potato Sack

**Players:** 1–16
**Skills:** Story sentences, throwing
**Age:** 3 and up
**Home use:** Yes
**Time:** 5–15 minutes
**You need:** A beanbag

Put the Story Sentence cards you want to practice on the floor in a "pool." Tape a line on the floor or use a rope that students must stand behind. Students stand behind this line and take turns tossing a beanbag (or "sack") into the "pool." If the beanbag

lands on a card, the student says the sentence and takes the card. Continue until all the cards are gone.

### Game 3: Potato Footsteps

**Players:** 2–16
**Skills:** Fluency
**Age:** 5 and up
**Home use:** Yes
**Time:** 5–10 minutes
**You need:** A fairly large space

Make a line of students against one wall of the room. Stand at the other end of the room, facing the students. Turn around, face the wall, and slowly say *At the store, we get a cart.* Students must try to get to you without being seen to move. They can only move when your back is turned.

After you say the sentence, quickly turn around. If you catch any students still moving, they must go back to the wall. The first student who makes it all the way to the front becomes the next caller. Change the sentence each time there is a new round.

**NOTE:** Teach your students to say *You moved!* or *Go back to the wall, please!*

 **More Practice**

**Pages 2–3 in the *Activity Book* and *Workbook* can be used with this lesson. The pages can be done in the classroom or as homework. Please check the answer key on page 89 for *Activity Book* and page 91 for *Workbook*.**

# A2 Focus Words

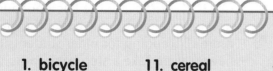

| 1. bicycle | 11. cereal |
|---|---|
| 2. cart | 12. tomato |
| 3. onion | 13. cookies |
| 4. carrots | 14. melon |
| 5. cabbage | 15. money |
| 6. bananas | 16. cheese |
| 7. orange | 17. chocolate |
| 8. grapes | 18. lemon |
| 9. bread | 19. watermelon |
| 10. milk | 20. motorcycle |

| |
|---|
| We get a cart: **bicycle, cart** |
| We go inside: **onion, carrots, cabbage** |
| We look for things: **bananas, orange, grapes** |
| We fill the cart: **bread, milk, cereal** |
| We wait in line: **tomato, cookies, melon** |
| We pay: **money, cheese** |
| We put things in bags: **chocolate, lemon** |
| We load the car: **watermelon, motorcycle** |

**OPTION:** There are other words in the pictures that you can also teach to extend the lesson. Some of these words appear as Focus Words for other books in Book Set 2.

| |
|---|
| We get a cart: **car, purse, baby** |
| We go inside: **door, cart** |
| We look for things: **clerk, apple, cans, box, pineapple, apron** |
| We fill the cart: **cherries, eggs, diapers, juice, honey, lemonade** |
| We wait in line: **yogurt** |
| We pay: **coin, coin purse, cash register** |
| We put things in bags: **pumpkin, poster, eggs, door** |
| We load the car: **purse, bags, trunk, road, rope, helmet, melon, bread** |

##  Potato Story Time

### Prediction

Show your students the cover of "At the Store," but do not open the book yet. Ask them to remember any of the objects they saw in the book. Help them by doing the movements for each sentence. Write the names and draw simple pictures of the objects they say on the board, even if the objects do not appear in the story.

 **QUICK TIP!** Hints are good! Write the first letter or say the first sound of a word to give students a little help, if they need it.

### Reading

After you read each sentence in "At the Store," point out the Focus Words listed below and ask students to repeat the words.

## Potato Activities

### Activity 1

Show the Focus Word picture cards, saying the words and clearly repeating them with the students. When the students are confident enough, you can ask one of them to "be the teacher"! That student then shows the cards and leads the class.

**NOTE:** You can use Reading 3 (Tracks 7–15) on the CD. Students will have fun finding the pictures of the words in the "Point and Say" practice.

### Activity 2

List the Focus Words on the board. Give each student a piece of paper and a pencil. Ask the students to draw one of the objects from the Focus Word list.

**OPTION:** Ask the students to draw other objects from the list by holding their pencils in the hand they don't always use, drawing with their eyes closed, drawing the object in 5 seconds, or drawing with another student with only one pencil. Try your own fun ideas, too!

## 🎵 Potato Song Time

Play Track 16 on the CD and sing the song with the students while doing the movements. Display the Story Sentence picture cards so that the students can see them clearly. Sing the song again while pointing at the cards. As an option, students can take turns singing different lines of the song.

## 🏁 Potato Games

### Game 1: Potato Jigsaws

**Players:** 1 or more    **Home use:** Yes
**Skills:** Vocabulary    **Time:** 5–15 minutes
**Age:** 3 and up    **You need:** Cardboard, scissors

Make simple jigsaw puzzles of the vocabulary words you want to practice. (Students can make these themselves if they are able to use scissors.) Divide the pieces between the students in the group and have them do their puzzle together, or give each student an individual puzzle. Have races between teams to see which one can put the puzzle together first. You can also hide the pieces around the room for students to find. Make sure to say the words as much as possible.

### Game 2: Potato Relay

**Players:** 4 or more    **Home use:** Yes
**Skills:** Focus words    **Time:** 5–10 minutes
**Age:** 4 and up    **You need:** Picture cards 9–28

Divide the students into two teams and have them stand at the other end of the room behind a line on the floor. Put one pile of Focus Words picture cards on either side of you. One student from each team runs to you. Show them a card from the top of their pile. They must say the word on the card. Then they can run back to their team and the next player in line does the same until all the students have had a turn. This is a relay race, so the fastest team to finish wins.

### Game 3: Shopping Lists

**Players:** 1 or more    **Home use:** Yes
**Skills:** Vocabulary, memory    **Time:** 10–15 minutes
**Age:** 5 and up    **You need:** Shopping lists

Give each student a shopping list with four items on it. You can write the words or just draw pictures for students who can't read yet. Put all the picture cards for the items on the lists facedown on a desk or on the floor. Students take turns turning over cards. If they turn over a card that is on their shopping list, they can keep it. If they turn over a card that is not on their list, they must turn it facedown again and it is the next student's turn. The first person to "buy" all the items on their list wins.

**NOTE:** You can have as many extra cards as you like, depending on how difficult you want to make this game. Encourage students to say the words as much as possible. Also teach them *I'm looking for _, Oh, yes!, Oh, no!,* and *You're lucky!*

### More Practice

**Pages 4–5 in the *Activity Book* and *Workbook* can be used with this lesson. The pages can be done in the classroom or as homework. Please check the answer key on page 89 for *Activity Book* and page 91 for *Workbook*.**

# Topic Words

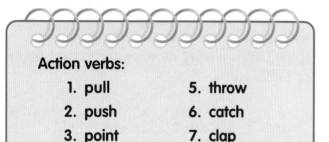

**Action verbs:**

1. pull
2. push
3. point
4. shake

5. throw
6. catch
7. clap
8. carry

##  Potato Story Time

### Prediction

Ask your students to tell you as many verbs as they know. Ask them what they like to do. Talk about the things that they did today.

### Reading

After you read the sentence on each page of "At the Store," point and ask *What can the baby do?* Help them with the answers and repeat together.

1. *She can pull.*
2. *She can push.*
3. *She can point.*
4. *She can shake.*

5. *She can throw.*
6. *She can catch.*
7. *She can clap.*
8. *She can carry.*

## Potato Activities

### Activity 1

Show and say the Topic Word picture cards for the verbs (Cards 29–36). Mix the cards, show them again, and ask *What can the baby do?* or *What can you do?* Students answer *She can (point), I can (point).* Give a card to each student, saying the verb as you give it. Then say *(Push), please,* and the student(s) with the card will give it back to you.

### Activity 2

Say a verb from "At the Store." Play the "At the Store" song. Students move around the room miming that verb. When you stop the music, they must freeze. The last student to stop moving gets an "out." If students get 3 outs, they must sit down.

**NOTE:** You can use this activity to practice the Story Sentences or any other verbs that you can mime. For larger groups, reduce the number of outs.

##  Potato Song Time

Play Track 16 on the CD and sing the song with the students while doing the movements. Display the Story Sentence picture cards so that the students can see them clearly. Sing the song again while pointing at the cards. As an option, students can take turns singing different lines of the song.

**QUICK TIP!** You can make students "take a rest" for a turn after they answer, allowing other students to catch up. If students can't say the whole phrase, give them hints by saying part of it for them and have them finish the phrase.

# Potato Games

## Game 1: Missing Potatoes

**Players:** 1–20
**Skills:** Memory
**Age:** 5 and up
**Home use:** Yes
**Time:** 3 minutes per round
**You need:** Picture cards 29–36

Attach the Topic Word picture cards to the board while saying the words with your students. Ask your students to face away from the board. Remove a card and hide it behind your back. Students turn around and look at the board. Give the card to the student who can say which card is missing. Continue until all the cards are gone.

## Game 2: Potato Circles

**Players:** 8–20
**Skills:** Miming and remembering verbs
**Age:** 4 and up
**Home use:** No
**Time:** 10 minutes
**You need:** Picture cards 29–36

Show the students the picture cards for the Topic Words and mime the verbs. Teach them *What can you do? I can (pull).* Put students into two circles of the same number of students, one inside the other. Each student from the inside circle should face a student from the outside circle. The inside student asks the outside student *What can you do?* The outside student mimes one of the Topic Words and says *I can (pull).* Continue for as long as you like, but change roles halfway though.

**NOTE:** This game is especially good for very large groups.

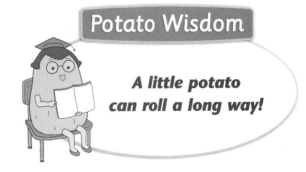

## Potato Wisdom

*A little potato can roll a long way!*

## Game 3: Dean Says

**Players:** 4–20
**Skills:** Physical response, miming
**Age:** 5 and up
**Home use:** Yes
**Time:** 10–15 minutes
**You need:** Picture cards 1–8

Students stand in a big circle. Show the Story Sentence cards and repeat the sentences while doing the actions. Explain that you are going to do an action from "At the Store." Tell the students that they must do the action, but only if you say *Dean says* before it. If you don't say *Dean says*, they should do nothing. If they make a move when you haven't said *Dean says*, they must sit down. Play until only one student is standing.

**NOTES:** For small groups, students can have more than one "out." For more advanced students, you can use different movements for the Story Sentences to make the game more difficult.

## More Practice

Pages 6–7 in the *Activity Book* and *Workbook* can be used with this lesson. The pages can be done in the classroom or as homework. Please check the answer key on page 89 for *Activity Book* and page 91 for *Workbook*.

ℰ =

# Review

##  Potato Story Time

### Prediction

Prompt your students to say the Story Sentences from the book by doing the actions from page 18. Ask them to tell you any Focus Words that they can remember. Elicit some of the Topic Words by asking students to mime and say verbs.

### Reading

Encourage your students to read the sentences themselves. Point out Focus Words. Ask *What can the baby do?* on each page.

##  Potato Activities

### Activity 1

Make a simple book and ask students to write a story about something that they did with their families. Encourage them to draw colorful pictures. A good way to get ideas flowing is to ask students for a lot of ideas at the beginning of this activity. Write or draw students' ideas on the board.

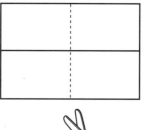
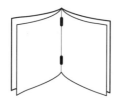

### Activity 2

Set up the classroom like a store, with tables acting as store shelves and display stands.

Put the Focus Word cards on the tables or, if they are available, use real fruits and vegetables. You can also have students make "products" out of recycled materials. Ask a few students to be "staff" and the rest to be "shoppers." Have students take turns "shopping." Set up role-plays. Student A says *I'm looking for (oranges). Can I have (an orange), please?* Student B answers *Here you are.* Student A says *Thank you.* Make some pretend money and have students ask *How much is/are this/these?* Play the "At the Store" song while you are playing the game.

**NOTE:** This kind of free play can be very creative and a really good way to practice the target language. Don't let things get too wild, though, and remember to speak as much as possible. Have students repeat what you say and help them to make up their own sentences.

## Potato Song Time

Play Track 16 on the CD and sing the song with the students while doing the movements. Display the Story Sentence picture cards so that the students can see them clearly. Sing the song again while pointing at the cards. As an option, students can take turns singing different lines of the song.

## Potato Games

### Game 1: Arrows!

**Players:** 2–4 per board
**Skills:** Reviewing all Book A language
**Age:** 5 and over
**Home use:** Yes
**Time:** 10–20 minutes
**You need:** Photocopies of the "Arrows!" game board on page 80, a die, game pieces

Copy the Focus Words, Topic Words and Story Sentence picture cards that you want to practice into some of the blank spaces on the game board. You don't need to fill them all.

Players put their game pieces on START. The youngest player rolls the die and moves his/her game piece that number of spaces. If the student lands directly on an arrow space, he/she must follow the direction of that arrow on the next turn. If the student lands on a word or sentence space and can say the word or sentence, he/she may roll the die again.

**NOTE:** Students might enjoy decorating the game board like a store. You can modify this game board to practice the language from any of the readers.

## Game 2: Puffing Potatoes

**Players:** 2–16
**Skills:** Reviewing all Book A language
**Age:** 4 and up
**Home use:** No
**Time:** 5–15 minutes
**You need:** Picture cards 1–36, scissors, paper

Have the students draw a simple shopping cart on a piece of paper. They can color it and cut it out. It should be about the size of a CD. Make a starting line on the floor and a "cash register" such as a desk or a chair (anything will do!).

Have all the students line up behind the starting line and place their carts on the floor in front of them. The object of the game is for students to move their cart from the starting line to the goal by blowing it along the floor.

Show students a card that you want to practice. The first student to tell you the word may give their cart one blow. The student to reach the cash register first is the winner.

**NOTE:** Challenge more advanced students (or good blowers!) by having them start farther away from the goal.

## Game 3: Potato, Paper, Scissors

**Players:** 2–20
**Skills:** Reviewing all Book A language
**Age:** 5 and up
**Home use:** Yes
**Time:** 5–15 minutes
**You need:** Picture cards 1–36

Divide the students into two teams. Show the students the Story Sentence, Focus Word, and Topic Word cards as you put them faceup on the floor in a straight line. Position one team at each end of the line of cards.

Teach the students how to play Rock, Paper, Scissors. When you say *Start!* one student from each team starts to make their way along the line of cards saying the words. When they meet in the middle, they do Rock, Paper, Scissors.

The winner of Rock, Paper, Scissors continues down the line towards the other team. The loser goes to the back of his/her team's line and the next student starts. The round is finished when a player gets all the way to the other team's end of the line.

## More Practice

Page 8 in the *Activity Book* and *Workbook* can be used with this lesson. The pages can be done in the classroom or as homework. Please check the answer key on page 89 for *Activity Book* and page 91 for *Workbook*.

# Color, cut, and stick.

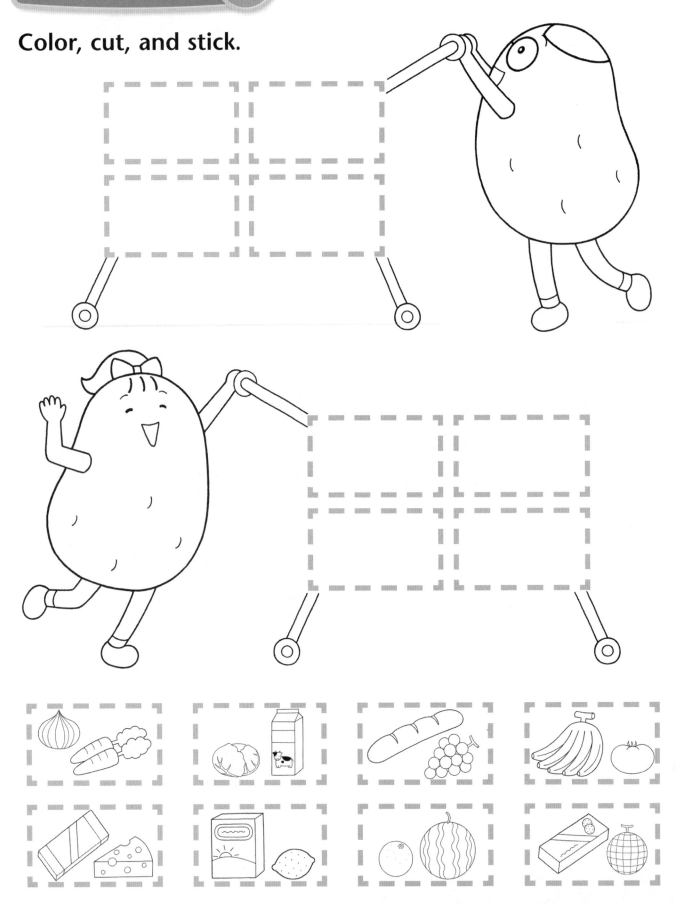

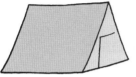

# At a Glance

## Book B: On a Camping Trip

### Story Sentences

On a camping trip, we ride in the car.
On a camping trip, we go hiking.
On a camping trip, we put up our tent.
On a camping trip, we go fishing.
On a camping trip, we have a barbecue.
On a camping trip, we sing songs.
On a camping trip, we count the stars.
On a camping trip, we say "Good night!"

### Focus Words

| | |
|---|---|
| 1. leaves | 11. corn |
| 2. mountain | 12. hot dog |
| 3. backpack | 13. guitar |
| 4. turtle | 14. squirrel |
| 5. tent | 15. fire |
| 6. fish | 16. owl |
| 7. river | 17. fox |
| 8. fishing rod | 18. star |
| 9. salad | 19. flashlight |
| 10. chicken | 20. sky |

### Topic Words

Adjectives:

| | |
|---|---|
| 1. fast | 5. big |
| 2. slow | 6. small |
| 3. new | 7. bright |
| 4. old | 8. dark |

### 🎵 Lyrics

"On a Camping Trip"

*Chorus:*
　　Camping, camping
　　Let's go camping!
　　Camping, camping, camping!

On a camping trip, we ride in the car
On a camping trip, we go hiking
On a camping trip, we put up our tent
On a camping trip, we go fishing

We ride in the car, we go hiking
We put up our tent, we go fishing
We ride in the car, we go hiking
We put up our tent, we go fishing

　　*Chorus*

On a camping trip, we have a barbecue
On a camping trip, we sing songs
On a camping trip, we count the stars
On a camping trip, we say "Good night!"

We have a barbecue, we sing songs
We count the stars, we say "Good night!"
We have a barbecue, we sing songs
We count the stars, we say "Good night!"

Good night, good night!
Good night, good night!

###  Picture Cards

Use Picture Cards 37–44 (Story Sentences),
45–64 (Focus Words), and 65–72 (Topic Words).

###  CD

Track numbers 17–30 (song is on Track 30)

On a camping trip, we ride in the car.
On a camping trip, we go hiking.
On a camping trip, we put up our tent.
On a camping trip, we go fishing.
On a camping trip, we have a barbecue.
On a camping trip, we sing songs.
On a camping trip, we count the stars.
On a camping trip, we say "Good night!"

##  Potato Story Time

### Prediction

Look at the cover of "On A Camping Trip" together. Explain to the students that this is a story about Daisy's family going camping. Ask the students if they have ever been camping or gone away for a night with their family. Focus students on things that they might do or have done on a camping trip.

### Reading

Read "On a Camping Trip" or play Tracks 17–18 of the CD. Use the Memoricons (see page 6) and have your students repeat as many of the sentences or parts of the sentences as they can.

**NOTE:** Do not expect too much from this first reading. Your students will probably only be able to repeat bits and pieces. Praise their efforts!

## 🕐 Potato Activities

### Activity 1

Show the eight Story Sentence picture cards one at a time. Mime the sentences for your students and then do them together:

1. We ride in the car. (Pretend to be steering a car.)

2. We go hiking. (March along, carrying a backpack.)

3. We put up our tent. (Put your hands together to form a tent shape.)

4. We go fishing. (Pretend to hold a fishing rod and reel in a big fish.)

5. We have a barbecue. (Pretend to cook food on a hot barbecue.)

6. We sing songs. (Play a guitar and sing.)

7. We count the stars. (Point out stars in the sky excitedly.)

8. We say "Good night!" (Put your hands to the side of your face and close your eyes.)

Now ask individual students to mime the sentences and have the other students say what they are doing.

### Activity 2

Show your students the Story Sentence cards 37–44 and have them repeat the sentences while doing the actions. Tell the students that they are the camp leaders and that you are on a camping trip and will do anything they say. They will enjoy ordering you to do the sentences from the book. When you have done this for a few minutes, put the students into pairs and make one the teacher and the other the student.

**NOTE:** Change roles often. Nobody likes to be told what to do all the time!

## ♫ Potato Song Time

Play Track 30 on the CD and sing the song with the students while doing the movements. Display the Story Sentence picture cards so that the students can see them clearly. Sing the song again while pointing at the cards. As an option, students can take turns singing different lines of the song.

**QUICK TIP!** The last page of "On A Camping Trip" shows all eight Memoricons. Students can point to them as they sing.

## Potato Games

### Game 1: Roll-a-Potato

**Players:** 4 or more
**Skills:** Story Sentences, rolling a ball
**Age:** 4 and up
**Home use:** Yes
**Time:** 5 minutes
**You need:** Picture cards 37–44, a ball

Students sit in a circle and roll a ball to each other, saying the first Story Sentence, *We ride in the car*. When they have practiced enough, show them the next card, *We go hiking*. Continue like this until they have said all the cards. Then show cards at random and ask individual students to say the sentences. If they can say the sentence, they can roll the ball. If they can't, they must give the ball to the student on their left and skip a turn.

**NOTE:** Help weaker students so that everyone has a chance to roll the ball. You can make the activity more challenging by putting some empty plastic bottles in the middle of the circle. Students must not knock over the bottles as they roll the ball.

## Game 2: Potatomime

**Players:** 4–16
**Skills:** Miming, Story Sentences
**Home use:** Yes
**Time:** 5–15 minutes
**Age:** 5 and up
**You need:** Picture cards 37–44

Divide the students into two teams. Show and say the Story Sentence picture cards. Show a student a card without the other students seeing it. The student mimes the sentence. The first team to call out the sentence gets a point. Choose another student to mime the next sentence. Gradually reduce the time limit after each round. Play until one team has reached a certain number of points.

**NOTE:** Some students will be shy about miming. Make it easy for them by doing the mimes with them until they are comfortable.

## Game 3: Hot Potatoes

**Players:** 2 or more   **Home use:** Yes
**Skills:** Fluency   **Time:** As long as you like
**Age:** 3 and up   **You need:** Any soft ball, a timer

Set a kitchen timer for one minute or use the classroom clock. Students make a circle and pass a ball around saying *On a camping trip, we ride in the car* until the timer goes off. The student holding the ball at that time leaves the circle. Continue, saying a different sentence each time until there is only one student.

**OPTION:** Give students more "outs." For 6–12 students, give each student 3 outs. For big groups, give each student 2 outs.

### More Practice

**Pages 9–10 in the *Activity Book* and *Workbook* can be used with this lesson. The pages can be done in the classroom or as homework. Please check the answer key on page 89 for *Activity Book* and page 91 for *Workbook*.**

# Focus Words

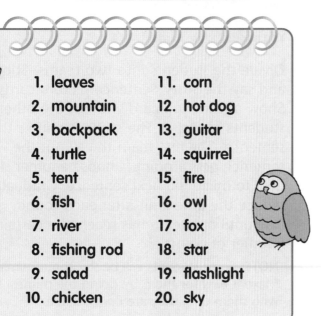

1. leaves
2. mountain
3. backpack
4. turtle
5. tent
6. fish
7. river
8. fishing rod
9. salad
10. chicken
11. corn
12. hot dog
13. guitar
14. squirrel
15. fire
16. owl
17. fox
18. star
19. flashlight
20. sky

| We ride in the car: **leaves, mountain** |
|---|
| We go hiking: **backpack, turtle** |
| We put up our tent: **tent** |
| We go fishing: **fish, river, fishing rod** |
| We have a barbecue: **salad, chicken, corn, hot dog** |
| We sing songs: **guitar, squirrel, fire** |
| We count the stars: **owl, fox, star** |
| We say "Good night!": **flashlight, sky** |

**OPTION:** There are other words in the pictures that you can also teach to extend the lesson. Some of these words appear as Focus Words for other books in Book Set 2.

| We ride in the car: **car, sunrise, steering wheel, headlights, safety belts, trees** |
|---|
| We go hiking: **clouds, trail, waterfall, trees, sign, box, fishing rod, boots, hat, sun** |
| We put up our tent: **rope, bird, chicks, box, instructions, stakes, nest, trees, mountain** |
| We go fishing: **boot, dragonfly, bucket, rocks, tackle box** |
| We have a barbecue: **smoke, fish, steak, sausage, knife, fork, dish, tablecloth, table, glass, ketchup, sunset** |
| We sing songs: **lantern, moths, music notes, logs, acorn** |
| We count the stars: **shooting star, telescope** |
| We say "Good night!": **sleeping bag, tent, trees, river, stars** |

##  Potato Story Time

### Prediction

Show your students the cover of "On a Camping Trip," but do not open the book yet. Ask them to remember any of the objects they saw in the book. Help them by doing the movements for each sentence. Write the names and draw simple pictures of the objects they say on the board, even if the objects do not appear in the story.

> **QUICK TIP!** Hints are good! Write the first letter or say the first sound of a word to give students a little help, if they need it.

### Reading

After you read each sentence in "On a Camping Trip," point out the Focus Words listed below and ask students to repeat the words.

##  Potato Activities

### Activity 1

Show the Focus Word picture cards, saying the words and clearly repeating them with the students. When the students are confident enough, you can ask one of them to "be the teacher"! That student then shows the cards and leads the class.

**NOTE:** You can use Reading 3 (Tracks 21–29) on the CD. Students will have fun finding the pictures of the words in the "Point and Say" practice.

## Activity 2

Show, say, and repeat the Focus Word picture cards. Turn one of the cards upside down. Show the cards again and have students repeat the words again. When you come to the upside-down card, the students have to stand up and say a sentence from the book. Continue in this way, putting a different card or cards upside down each time.

## Potato Song Time

Play Track 30 on the CD and sing the song with the students while doing the movements. Display the Story Sentence picture cards so that the students can see them clearly. Sing the song again while pointing at the cards. As an option, students can take turns singing different lines of the song.

## Potato Games

### Game 1: Potato Grab

**Players:** 2–8
**Skills:** Vocabulary
**Age:** 3 and up
**Home use:** Yes
**Time:** 5–15 minutes
**You need:** Picture cards 45–64

Arrange the Focus Word cards faceup in a "pool" either on the floor or on a table. Students stand around the "pool." Say a word. The first student to touch the card with the word can keep it. The student with the most cards at the end of the game is the winner.

You can vary this game by asking your students to start with their hands on their heads or behind their backs, or have them face the other way.

**NOTE:** Make sure that the bigger students do not control the game. Call out some cards that are closer to smaller students.

### Game 2: Potato Pieces

**Players:** 1–20
**Skills:** Vocabulary
**Age:** 3 and up
**Home use:** Yes
**Time:** 5–15 minutes
**You need:** A board or paper

Divide the class into teams. Start drawing part of one of the vocabulary words on the board. Slowly draw more and more as students guess what you are drawing. The team that guesses first gets a point. Play until you have drawn all the words.

**NOTE:** For more advanced students, you can play a version of this game where you write the word letter by letter—but not always starting with the first letter!

### Game 3: Potato!

**Players:** 2 or more
**Skills:** Recognizing vocabulary
**Age:** 3 and up
**Home use:** Yes
**Time:** 15 minutes
**You need:** Photocopied "Potato!" sheets (page 78), picture cards 45–64

Photocopy one "Potato!" sheet for each student. Show the Focus Word picture cards. Say the words and repeat. Place the cards somewhere the students can see them. Students draw or write the words on their Potato! sheets at random. When they have completed their sheets, shuffle the cards and call the words out one at a time. Students circle the words you call out, saying *I found it!* As in Bingo, the first student to get a line of potatoes calls out *Potato!* You can play for vertical, horizontal, or diagonal lines.

### More Practice

Pages 11–12 in the *Activity Book* and *Workbook* can be used with this lesson. The pages can be done in the classroom or as homework. Please check the answer key on page 89 for *Activity Book* and page 91 for *Workbook*.

# LESSON B3 — Topic Words

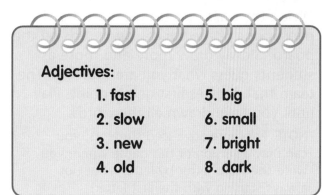

**Adjectives:**

1. fast
2. slow
3. new
4. old
5. big
6. small
7. bright
8. dark

##  Potato Story Time

### Prediction

Ask students to tell you any adjectives they know. Prompt them by miming and asking *What's a ~ like?* (for various objects that they know). Draw some groups of objects on the board.

### Reading

After you read the sentence on each page of "On a Camping Trip," point and ask *What's the (car) like?* Help the students with the answers and repeat together.

1. *It's fast.* (car)
2. *It's slow.* (turtle)
3. *It's new.* (tent)
4. *It's old.* (boot)
5. *It's big.* (corn)
6. *It's small.* (guitar)
7. *It's bright.* (shooting star)
8. *It's dark.* (sky)

 **QUICK TIP!** You can challenge students with Topic Words and Focus Words by asking questions about other words—for example, *What's a mountain like? It's big.*

## 🕐 Potato Activities

### Activity 1

Show your students the Topic Word cards and ask *What's it like?* after you show each one. Give out a card to each student, saying the adjective word as you hand it to them. Then say *(Fast), please,* and have the students give the cards back to you. Practice the adjectives by asking your students *What's a bus like?* or by pointing to pictures or objects in the classroom and asking *What's this like?* As soon as possible, encourage your students to ask each other the questions.

### Activity 2

Start a word network like this on the board.

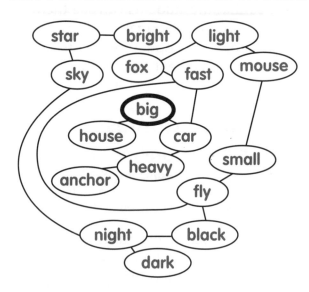

See how far you can expand the network and remember that objects can be described in more than one way. For example, a bus is big and fast.

**NOTE:** Younger pre-reading students may need pictures as well as the words.

## 🎵 Potato Song Time

Play Track 30 on the CD and sing the song with the students while doing the movements. Display the Story Sentence picture cards so that the students can see them clearly. Sing the song again while pointing at the cards. As an option, students can take turns singing different lines of the song.

## Potato Games

### Game 1: Potato Camping Trip

**Players:** 2–20
**Skills:** Remembering adjectives
**Age:** 3 and up
**Home use:** Yes
**Time:** 5–10 minutes
**You need:** Small pieces of paper shaped like acorns and nuts, picture cards 65–72

Explain to the students that they are squirrels in the forest gathering acorns. They will get lots of nuts and acorns if they can say the Topic Words. Practice once by saying and repeating the words with them. Make a "hiking trail" through the "forest" (a group of chairs). Sit at one point (the "big tree") and show children the Topic Word cards as they go past you. If they can say the word on the card, give them a "nut" and repeat the word. If they can't, tell them the word again. The students move around the tree collecting as many nuts and acorns as they can.

### Game 2: Potato and Spoon Race

**Players:** Teams of 4–8
**Skills:** Vocabulary, balance
**Age:** 4 and up
**Home use:** Yes
**Time:** 5–15 minutes
**You need:** Picture cards 65–72, potatoes (or balls), spoons

Make teams of not more than eight students per team. Draw or tape a starting line on the floor and have teams line up behind it. Give the student at the front of each line a big spoon and a small potato (or table tennis ball). Have the students place the potatoes on the spoons. You sit in a chair on the opposite side of the room.

The object of the game is for students to reach you without dropping the potato. If the potato drops, they must go back and start again. Show each student who reaches you a card. The student must say the word on the card. Teams get one point for every correct answer.

This is a relay race, so when the students get back to their teams, they give the spoon and potato to the next player. The first team to complete a round wins.

### Game 3: Potato Chance!

**Players:** 2–20
**Skills:** Topic Words
**Age:** 4 and up
**Home use:** Yes
**Time:** 5–10 minutes
**You need:** Picture cards 65–72

Show, say, and repeat the Topic Words. Make groups of three noun picture cards for each adjective (for *slow* you could use *turtle*, *chicken*, and *owl*). Shuffle the noun cards and put them all around the room. Students go and stand by a card. Ask them *What is it? What's it like?* They answer *It's a (turtle). It's (slow).* Turn over a Topic Word card. The students standing next to a noun which matches the adjective get a point. Play to a time limit or up to a certain number of points.

**OPTION:** Use Focus Word cards from other Level 2 books that go well with the Book B adjectives (example: *motorcycle* [28] and *train* [99] for *fast*).

### More Practice

Pages 13–14 in the *Activity Book* and *Workbook* can be used with this lesson. The pages can be done in the classroom or as homework. Please check the answer key on page 89 for *Activity Book* and page 91 for *Workbook*.

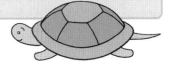

# LESSON B4 — Review

of the pages. Have an exhibition at the end of the lesson and talk about their pictures.

## Activity 2

Turn the classroom into a campsite using a sheet over a table or chairs to make a tent. Set up a barbecue and a campfire. Students will enjoy crawling along the floor between chair legs pretending that they're in a forest. Sing the "On a Camping Trip" song while you are playing.

**NOTE:** This kind of free play can be very creative and a really good way to practice the target language. Don't let things get too wild, though, and remember to speak as much as possible. Have students repeat what you say and help them to make up their own sentences.

##  Potato Story Time

### Prediction

Prompt your students to say the Story Sentences from the book by doing the actions from page 28. Ask them to tell you any Focus Words that they can remember. Elicit some of the Topic Words by asking students to name adjectives.

### Reading

Encourage your students to read the sentences themselves. Point out Focus Words. Ask *What is ~ like?* on each page. Be sure to review all of the Topic Words (adjectives). Ask about other objects in the pictures.

## Potato Activities

### Activity 1

Give each student tracing paper and have them trace some of the pages from "On a Camping Trip." Ask students to change some of the details in the picture. Students can have great fun making their own versions

## Potato Song Time

Play Track 30 on the CD and sing the song with the students while doing the movements. Display the Story Sentence picture cards so that the students can see them clearly. Sing the song again while pointing at the cards. As an option, students can take turns singing different lines of the song.

**Potato Games**

## Game 1: Potato Picking

**Players:** 2–12
**Skills:** Focus Words, Topic Words
**Age:** 6 and up
**Home use:** Yes
**Time:** 5–10 minutes
**You need:** Picture cards 45–72

Show, say, and repeat about 8 of the picture cards that you want to practice. Shuffle and place the cards facedown on the floor. Pick a student and say *Pick up ~, please.* The student turns over a card and says the word. If it is the card you asked for, the student can keep the card. If not, the student turns the card back over and another student gets a turn. Continue until all the cards are gone.

**NOTE:** You might have to give the students hints if they can't remember the cards. You can do this by drawing or writing words on the board.

## Game 2: Potato Mistake

**Players:** 2–20
**Skills:** Vocabulary
**Age:** 6 and up
**Home use:** Yes
**Time:** 5–10 minutes
**You need:** Picture cards 37–72

Students stand up. Show the Story Sentence, Focus Word, or Topic Word cards and have students repeat. Tell students that you will say them again, but you will make a mistake and say a word or sentence that is not on one of the cards. Tell them they cannot repeat it. If they do repeat the incorrect word or sentence, they must sit down. Play for a period of time or until there is only one student standing.

## Potato Wisdom

*Potatoes come in different sizes, but all of them are good!*

## Game 3: Potato Lines

**Players:** 6 or more
**Skills:** Vocabulary
**Age:** 3 and up
**Home use:** Yes
**Time:** 5–15 minutes
**You need:** Picture cards 45–64

Make two or more lines of students and show a Focus Word card to the first student in line. The student who says the card first runs to the back of his/her line. The other students stay at the front of their lines. The first team to do a complete "round" of all its students is the winner.

 **QUICK TIP!** If a student loses three times, give the student a free walk to the back of the line. This will keep the game moving and avoid putting too much pressure on the students who are not as quick.

## More Practice

**Page 15 in the *Activity Book* and *Workbook* can be used with this lesson. The pages can be done in the classroom or as homework. Please check the answer key on page 89 for *Activity Book* and page 91 for *Workbook*.**

# Worksheet **B**

## Color, cut, and stick.

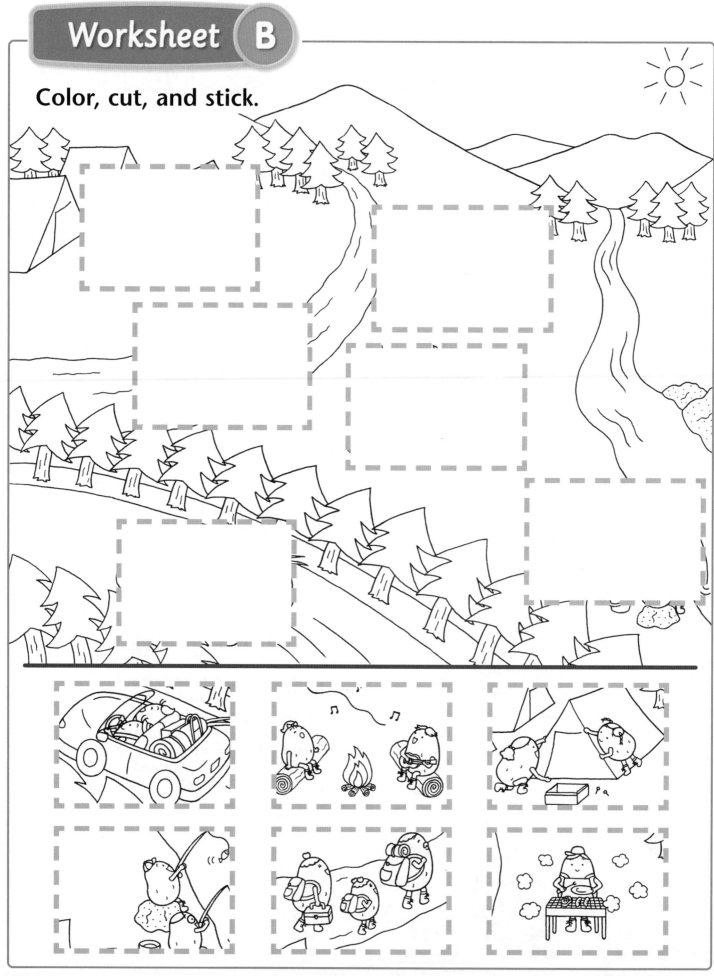

## At a Glance

### Book C: In Town

### Story Sentences

In town, we buy candy.
In town, we get haircuts.
In town, we mail letters.
In town, we shop for shoes.
In town, we borrow books.
In town, we go to a movie.
In town, we visit a museum.
In town, we eat at a restaurant.

### Focus Words

1. candy
2. balloon
3. candy store
4. barber shop
5. letter
6. post office
7. sandals
8. shoe store
9. purse
10. cell phone
11. library
12. popcorn
13. movie theater
14. museum
15. mouse
16. pizza
17. spaghetti
18. restaurant

### Topic Words

Vehicles:
1. train
2. ambulance
3. truck
4. taxi
5. airplane
6. helicopter
7. ship
8. fire engine

### Lyrics

"In Town"

*Chorus:*
>    In town!
>    In town!

In town, we buy candy
In town, we get haircuts
In town, we mail letters
In town, we shop for shoes

In town, we borrow books
In town, we go to a movie
In town, we visit a museum
In town, we eat at a restaurant

*Chorus*

In town, we buy candy
In town, we get haircuts
In town, we mail letters
In town, we shop for shoes

In town, we borrow books
In town, we go to a movie
In town, we visit a museum
In town, we eat at a restaurant

*Chorus*

### Picture Cards

Use Picture Cards 73–80 (Story Sentences),
81–98 (Focus Words), and 99–106
(Topic Words).

### CD

Track numbers 31–44 (song is on Track 44)

# C1 Story Sentences

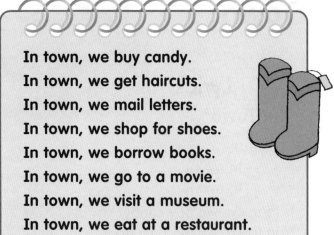

In town, we buy candy.
In town, we get haircuts.
In town, we mail letters.
In town, we shop for shoes.
In town, we borrow books.
In town, we go to a movie.
In town, we visit a museum.
In town, we eat at a restaurant.

1. We buy candy. (Unwrap and eat delicious candy.)
2. We get haircuts. (Move your fingers through your hair as if they were scissors.)
3. We mail letters. (Pretend to put a letter in a mailbox.)
4. We shop for shoes. (Point to beautiful new shoes.)
5. We borrow books. (Take a book off the shelf and pretend to take it out of the library.)
6. We go to a movie. (Mime a screen in front of you and look excited.)
7. We visit a museum. (Stroke your chin as if looking at something interesting.)
8. We eat at a restaurant. (Pretend to eat.)

Now ask individual students to mime the sentences and have the other students say what they are doing.

##  Potato Story Time

### Prediction

Look at the cover of "In Town" with the students. Focus the students on the things that they like to do in town. Ask them to tell you some of the shops one might find in a town. Where do they like going best? Explain that "In Town" is a book about what Chip likes to do with his friends in town.

### Reading

Read "In Town" or play Tracks 31 and 32 on the CD. Point to the Memoricons (see page 6) and have your students repeat as many of the sentences or parts of the sentences as they can.

**NOTE:** For this first reading, your students will probably only be able to repeat bits and pieces. Praise their efforts!

## ⏰ Potato Activities

### Activity 1

Show the eight Story Sentence picture cards one at a time. Mime the sentences for your students and then do them together:

## Activity 2

All the students make a circle. Pass the student on your left the card for *We buy candy* and say the sentence. The student passes the card to the next student to the left and repeats the sentence. Add more cards to the circle and have students pass them around faster and faster!

**OPTION:** Replace the cards with the mimed movements for the phrases.

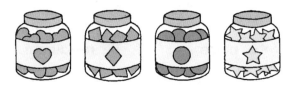

## 💿🎵 Potato Song Time

Play Track 44 on the CD and sing the song with the students while doing the movements. Display the Story Sentence picture cards so that the students can see them clearly. Sing the song again while pointing at the cards. As an option, students can take turns singing different lines of the song.

 **QUICK TIP!** The last page of "In Town" shows all eight Memoricons. Students can point to them as they sing.

## Potato Games

### Game 1: Potato Mail

**Players:** 2 or more
**Skills:** Story Sentences
**Age:** 3 and up
**Home use:** Yes
**Time:** 5–10 minutes
**You need:** A cardboard mailbox

Make a "mailbox" out of a cardboard box with a slot for putting cards in. (You can use this at any time for practicing any cards you like). Show, say, and repeat the picture cards for the Story Sentences. Show the cards again one at a time. This time, the student who says the card first gets to put the card in the mailbox.

**NOTE:** To make this game less competitive, have students take turns mailing the letters, but let the student who says the most words "deliver" them back to you by emptying the box and bringing the cards to you.

### Game 2: Going Home!

**Players:** 2–4 per board
**Skills:** Story Sentences
**Age:** 5 and up
**Home use:** Yes
**Time:** 10–15 minutes
**You need:** Photocopied game board on page 79, a die, some game pieces

Draw the Story Sentence icons in the "houses" on the game board. (Students can do this themselves if you display the picture cards where they can see them.) Students place their game pieces at START. The youngest player starts and rolls the die. When the student comes to a "house," he/she says the Story Sentence and passes the die to the next player. The first player to reach home is the winner.

**NOTE:** You can ask higher level students to say all the previous sentences each time they come to a house. You can also make them go back to the previous house if they can't say the sentence.

### Game 3: Move On!

**Players:** 2–16
**Skills:** Sentence practice
**Age:** 4 and up
**Home use:** Yes
**Time:** 5–10 minutes
**You need:** A picture card from 73–80 for each student

Put the Story Sentence cards in various places around the room where students can see them. As you place the cards, be sure to say, mime, and repeat the phrases. Assign a student to each card. Students take turns saying and miming the sentence on their cards. When you say *Move on!*, students change cards and take turns saying and miming their new sentences.

**NOTE:** If you have more than one student per card, they can say the sentence together. This is a non-competitive game, but if you want to make it competitive, give students points if they can say the sentences correctly.

## More Practice

**Pages 16–17 in the *Activity Book* and *Workbook* can be used with this lesson. The pages can be done in the classroom or as homework. Please check the answer key on page 89 for *Activity Book* and page 91 for *Workbook*.**

# Focus Words

1. candy
2. balloon
3. candy store
4. barber shop
5. letter
6. post office
7. sandals
8. shoe store
9. purse
10. cell phone
11. library
12. popcorn
13. movie theater
14. museum
15. mouse
16. pizza
17. spaghetti
18. restaurant

## 📖 Potato Story Time

### Prediction

Show your students the cover of "In Town," but do not open the book yet. Ask them to remember any of the objects or places they saw in the book. Write the names and draw simple pictures of the objects they say on the board, even if they are do not appear in the book.

### Reading

After you read each sentence in "In Town," point out the Focus Words listed below and ask students to repeat the words.

| | |
|---|---|
| We buy candy: | **candy, balloon, candy store** |
| We get haircuts: | **barber shop** |
| We mail letters: | **letter, post office** |
| We shop for shoes: | **sandals, shoe store** |
| We borrow books: | **purse, cell phone, library** |
| We go to a movie: | **popcorn, movie theater** |
| We visit a museum: | **museum, mouse** |
| We eat at a restaurant: | **pizza, spaghetti, restaurant** |

**OPTION:** There are other words in the pictures that you can also teach to extend the lesson. Some of these words appear as Focus Words for other books in Book Set 2.

| |
|---|
| We buy candy: **clerk, cash register, jars, lollipops, square, circle, triangle, star, rectangle, diamond, heart, oval, apron, hat, shelf** |
| We get haircuts: **barbers, scissors, hairbrush, mirror, hairdryer, comb, cap** |
| We mail letters: **stamp, mailbox, mail carrier, package, sacks, cap, purse** |
| We shop for shoes: **price tag, boots, sneakers, slippers, shelf, door, taxi driver** |
| We borrow books: **books, librarian, shelves, deer** |
| We go to a movie: **seats, mountain, snow, ladder, drink, exit** |
| We visit a museum: **sculpture, painting, sea, pirate, flag** |
| We eat at a restaurant: **chicken, steak, juice, hamburger, hot dog, dishes, glasses, hose, ladder, table, menu, waiter** |

## 🕐 Potato Activities

### Activity 1

Show the Focus Word picture cards, saying the words and clearly repeating them with the students. When the students are confident enough, you can ask one of them to "be the teacher"! That student then shows the cards and leads the class.

**NOTE:** You can use Reading 3 (Tracks 35–43) on the CD. Students will have fun finding the pictures of the words in the "Point and Say" practice.

### Activity 2

List the Focus Words on the board. Give each student a piece of paper and a pencil. Ask the students to draw one of the objects from the Focus Word list.

**OPTION:** See the top of page 21 for other options that can be used with this activity.

# ♫ Potato Song Time

Play Track 44 on the CD and sing the song with the students while doing the movements. Display the Story Sentence picture cards so that the students can see them clearly. Sing the song again while pointing at the cards. As an option, students can take turns singing different lines of the song.

# Potato Games

## Game 1: Blindfold Go!

**Players:** 2 and up
**Skills:** Focus Words, following instructions
**Age:** 6 and over
**Home use:** Yes
**Time:** 10–15 minutes
**You need:** A blindfold, picture cards 83, 84, 86, 88, 91, 93, 95, 98

Show, say, and repeat the words on the picture cards listed above. Position the cards around the room to make a "town." Teach the students how to say *left*, *right*, *straight*, *back*, and *stop*. Show the students what the words mean. Put on the blindfold and have students give you directions to get to certain places. When they are confident in giving directions, it's their turn. Blindfold a student. Say the name of a place. The other students must give the blindfolded student directions to that place. For older students, this game can be played in teams with two blindfolded players listening to their own team's directions. Be prepared for confusion!

> **NOTE:** As with all blindfold games, take great care! Remove any dangerous objects from the playing area. Stay close to the blindfolded student at all times. You may have to help guide the students or help students who get lost.

## Game 2: Missing Potatoes

**Players:** 1–16
**Skills:** Vocabulary, throwing
**Age:** 3 and up
**Home use:** Yes
**Time:** 5–15 minutes
**You need:** A beanbag

Put the Focus Words cards you want to practice on the floor in a "pool." Tape a line on the floor or use a rope that students must stand behind. Students stand behind this line and take turns tossing a beanbag into the "pool." If the beanbag lands on a card, the student says the word and takes the card. Continue until all the cards are gone.

## Game 3: Potato, Paper, Scissors

**Players:** 2–20
**Skills:** Vocabulary
**Age:** 5 and up
**Home use:** Yes
**Time:** 5–15 minutes
**You need:** Picture cards 73–106

Divide the students into two teams. Show the students the picture cards as you put them faceup on the floor in a straight line. Position one team at each end of the line of cards.

Teach the students how to play Rock, Paper, Scissors. When you say *Start!* one student from each team starts to make their way along the line of cards saying the words. When they meet in the middle, they do Rock, Paper, Scissors.

The winner of Rock, Paper, Scissors continues down the line towards the other team. The loser goes to the back of his/her team's line and the next student starts. The round is finished when a player gets all the way to the other team's end of the line.

## More Practice

Pages 18–19 in the *Activity Book* and *Workbook* can be used with this lesson. The pages can be done in the classroom or as homework. Please check the answer key on page 90 for *Activity Book* and page 91 for *Workbook*.

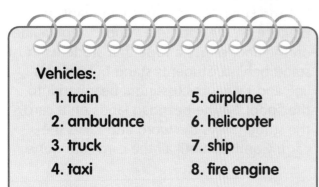

Vehicles:
1. train
2. ambulance
3. truck
4. taxi
5. airplane
6. helicopter
7. ship
8. fire engine

##  Potato Story Time

### Prediction

Ask students what vehicles they know. Find out which vehicles they have ridden. How do they get around? How did they come here today? What vehicles would they *like* to ride?

### Reading

After you read each sentence in "In Town," point to the picture and ask *What vehicle can you see?* Help students find them and repeat together.

1. *I see a train.*
2. *I see an ambulance.*
3. *I see a truck.*
4. *I see a taxi.*
5. *I see an airplane.*
6. *I see a helicopter.*
7. *I see a ship.*
8. *I see a fire engine.*

## 🕐 Potato Activities

### Activity 1

Give each student a Topic Word (*vehicle*) card and tell them that they are going to be that vehicle. Make some "roads" around the room, between the desks and even under tables. Encourage students to make the noises of their vehicles!

Make a big red and a big green circle out of paper and pretend to be the traffic light. Say *Go!* and show the green light. Students move around as their vehicle. When you say *Stop!* and show the red light, students must stop moving. The last student to stop moving gets an out. Ask students *What vehicle are you?* They say what vehicle they are and change cards with another student. If they get three outs, they must sit down.

**NOTE:** You can use this activity to practice the Story Sentences or any verbs that you can mime. For larger groups, reduce the number of outs.

### Activity 2

Show, say, and repeat all the Topic Word cards for "In Town." Pass the cards around the group and have students say the card that is in their hands. Then show the cards as fast as you can to the whole group. Give the card to the student who can say the word first.

## 💿🎵 Potato Song Time

Play Track 44 on the CD and sing the song with the students while doing the movements. Display the Story Sentence picture cards so that the students can see them clearly. Sing the song again while pointing at the cards. As an option, students can take turns singing different lines of the song.

 # Potato Games

## Game 1: Potato Train

**Players:** 3–16
**Skills:** Vocabulary practice
**Age:** 4–8
**Home use:** Yes
**Time:** 5–10 minutes
**You need:** Scissors, paper, picture cards 99–106

You will need to make some small slips of scrap paper for this simple game. They can be potato-shaped. These will be the "Potato Train Tickets."

Make a "train track" around the classroom with tables and chairs. This is the track that students go around. Sit down at one point along the track. You are the Stationmaster and this is Potato Central Station.

Students make a line (the "train") and move around the track. Every time the train passes Potato Central Station, it must stop. You, the Stationmaster, must pick a student from the train. Show the student a card. If he/she can say the word or sentence on the card, give the student a Potato Train Ticket.

Play to a time limit. At the end of the time, count the tickets. The winner is the student with the most tickets.

## Game 2: Potato Skittles

**Players:** 2–16
**Skills:** Vocabulary practice, rolling a ball
**Age:** 3 and up
**Home use:** Yes
**Time:** 10 to make, 15 to play
**You need:** Carboard tubes or bottles, tennis ball

Make eight skittles (bowling pins) from cardboard paper towel tubes or milk cartons. Decorate them with pictures of the vehicle Topic Words. Divide the class into two or more teams. Select two students to be "umpires." Mark a line on the floor from behind which students will roll the ball. Students take turns rolling the ball and trying to knock over the pins. The umpires

replace the pins while showing them to the other students. Keep score by giving one point for each vehicle knocked over and said aloud. Play to a time limit or until one team has scored a certain number of points.

**NOTES:** Increase the number of pins by adding car, bicycle, bus, rocket, etc.

## Game 3: Potato Slap Clap

**Players:** 1–20
**Skills:** Fluency
**Age:** 4 and up
**Home use:** Yes
**Time:** 5–10 minutes
**You need:** Picture cards 99–106

Put the Topic Word cards on the board. Stand in a circle with students and model the following chant:

*Slap, slap, clap, clap,* **train, train**
*Slap, slap, clap, clap,* **ambulance, ambulance**
*Slap, slap, clap, clap,* **truck, truck**
*Slap, slap, clap, clap,* **taxi, taxi**
*Slap, slap, clap, clap,* **airplane, airplane**
*Slap, slap, clap, clap,* **helicopter, helicopter**
*Slap, slap, clap, clap,* **ship, ship**
*Slap, slap, clap, clap,* **fire engine, fire engine**

As you say *Slap,* slap your hands on your knees. As you say *clap,* clap your hands.

Do the chant again, but this time go around the circle with a different student saying the vehicle each time. Students have to keep the rhythm but cannot say the same vehicle as the student before them. If they can't say something in time, they are out of that round.

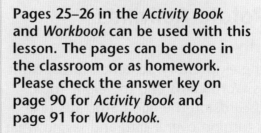
**More Practice**

**Pages 25–26** in the *Activity Book* and *Workbook* can be used with this lesson. The pages can be done in the classroom or as homework. Please check the answer key on **page 90** for *Activity Book* and **page 91** for *Workbook.*

## LESSON C4 Review

 **Potato Story Time**

### Prediction

Prompt your students to say the Story Sentences from the book by doing the actions from page 38. Ask them to tell you any Focus Words that they can remember. Elicit some of the Topic Words and write them on the board.

### Reading

Encourage your students to read the sentences themselves. Point out Focus Words. Ask *What vehicle is this?* on each page. Be sure to review all of the Topic Words (vehicles).

## 🕐 Potato Activities

### Activity 1

Put the eight Story Sentence cards, eight Focus Word cards and the eight Topic Word cards on the floor. Students take turns turning over a card and saying what is on the card. Students try to turn over two

of the same type of card—for example, two Focus Word cards. If they do, then they can keep the pair. If the cards are of a different type, they must be turned back over and it is the next student's turn. Make sure all the students say the words and sentences on the cards as much as possible. Continue until all the cards are off of the floor.

### Activity 2

Make a model town out of recycled materials. Include all the places from the book. Make vehicles and drive them around the town. This can be a major class project that takes several lessons. Make little human (or potato!) figures and play with them in their new town.

## 💿🎵 Potato Song Time

Play track 44 on the CD and sing the song with the students while doing the movements. Display the Story Sentence picture cards so that the students can see them clearly. Sign the song again while pointing at the cards. As an option, students can take turns singing different lines of the song.

## ▪️ Potato Games

### Game 1: Potato Roll
**Players:** 2–20
**Skills:** Story Sentences, counting
**Age:** 4 and up
**Home use:** Yes
**Time:** 10–15 minutes
**You need:** Two large homemade dice

Make a die out of recycled materials. You can use milk cartons or something similar. The die should be big enough for all the students to see when it is rolled. Decorate each side of the die with a Story Sentence Memoricon. Students take turns rolling the die and saying the sentences that come up. They get one point for each sentence they can say correctly. Keep score on the board and play to a time limit or up to a certain number of points. This game can be played as a team game.

**OPTION 1:** Add a number to each side of the die so that students get different amounts of points for different Story Sentences they can say. Use higher numbers for the sentences that are harder to say.

**OPTION 2:** Instead of Memoricons, you can put actions (such as *Stand on one leg for a minute*) on the die. This makes the game even more exciting!

## Game 2: Mashed Potatoes

**Players:** 2–12
**Skills:** Remembering language
**Age:** 4 and up
**Home use:** Yes
**Time:** 5–10 minutes
**You need:** Picture cards 73–106

Place the cards you want to practice faceup on the floor where all the students can see them. Secretly write one of the words or sentences on a piece of paper. Students take turns saying the words or sentences. When the word is said, the card is turned over. If a student chooses the word or sentence you have secretly written, he/she is "mashed" (out of the game). Each time this happens you turn all the cards faceup again and choose another word (it can be the same word!). Continue until only one student remains unmashed!

## Game 3: Missing Potatoes

**Players:** 2–20
**Skills:** Memory
**Age:** 4 and up
**Home use:** Yes
**Time:** 3 minutes per round
**You need:** Picture cards 73–80

Attach the Story Sentence picture cards to the board while saying the sentences with your students. Ask your students to face away from the board. Remove a card and hide it behind your back. Students turn around and look at the board. Give the card to the student who can say which card is missing. Continue until all the cards are gone.

**QUICK TIP!** You can make students "take a rest" for a turn after they answer, allowing other students to catch up. If students can't say the whole phrase, give them hints by saying part of it for them and just have them finish the phrase.

## More Practice

Page 22 in the *Activity Book* and *Workbook* can be used with this lesson. The pages can be done in the classroom or as homework. Please check the answer key on page 90 for *Activity Book* and page 91 for *Workbook*.

**Draw and color.**

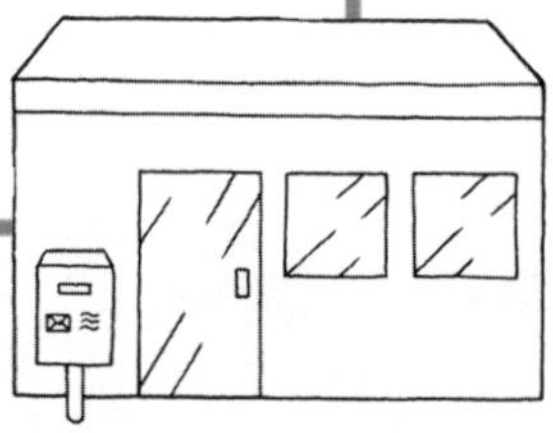

## My Town

I live in

_____

_____

_____

# At a Glance

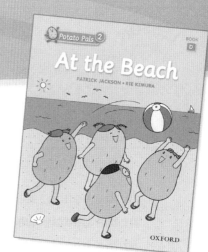

## Book D: At the Beach

### Story Sentences

At the beach, we put on sun block.
At the beach, we play in the sea.
At the beach, we build sand castles.
At the beach, we chase crabs.
At the beach, we swim.
At the beach, we go for a boat ride.
At the beach, we find shells.
At the beach, we have a picnic.

### Focus Words

1. sunglasses
2. sea
3. island
4. dolphin
5. sand castle
6. crab
7. net
8. seal
9. beach ball
10. whale
11. anchor
12. octopus
13. shark
14. shells
15. sandwich
16. peach
17. basket

### Topic Words

**Adjectives:**

1. far
2. near
3. long
4. short
5. light
6. heavy
7. full
8. empty

 **Lyrics**

**"At the Beach"**

*Chorus:*
At the beach
At the beach, beach, beach
At the beach
At the beach, beach, beach

We put on sun block
We play in the sea
We build sand castles
We chase crabs

*Chorus*

We swim
We go for a boat ride
We find shells
We have a great time!

*Chorus*

*Repeat all*

 **Picture Cards**

Use Picture Cards 107–114 (Story Sentences), 115–131 (Focus Words), and 132–139 (Topic Words).

 **CD**

Track numbers 45–58 (song is on Track 58)

## LESSON D1 Story Sentences

At the beach, we put on sun block.
At the beach, we play in the sea.
At the beach, we build sand castles.
At the beach, we chase crabs.
At the beach, we swim.
At the beach, we go for a boat ride.
At the beach, we find shells.
At the beach, we have a picnic.

###  Potato Story Time

#### Prediction

Look at the cover of "At the Beach" together. Explain to the students that this is a story about the things that Nina does with her family at the beach. Ask students if they have ever been to a beach, and if so, what they saw or did there. Write some of their answers on the board.

#### Reading

Read "At the Beach" or play Tracks 45 and 46 of the CD. Use the Memoricons (see page 6) and have your students repeat as many of the sentences or parts of the sentences as they can.

NOTE: Do not expect too much from this first reading. Your students will probably only be able to repeat bits and pieces. Praise their efforts!

###  Potato Activities

#### Activity 1

Show the eight Story Sentence picture cards one at a time. Mime the sentences for your students and then do them together:

1. We put on sun block. (Pour sun block from a bottle into your hand and rub it onto your arm.)
2. We play in the sea. (Pass a beach ball to a student.)
3. We build sand castles. (Kneel, dig, and pat a sand castle as if at the beach.)
4. We chase crabs. (Run in place, pretending to trap crabs in a net.)
5. We swim. (Move your arms as if swimming.)
6. We go for a boat ride. (Pretend you are on a boat. Put your hand to your forehead as if looking at the horizon.)
7. We find shells. (Pick up shells that you put in a bucket.)
8. We have a picnic. (Pretend to eat sandwiches.)

Now ask individual students to do the actions and have the other students say what they are doing.

#### Activity 2

Show, say, and repeat the Story Sentence cards. Pass the cards around the group and have students say the card that is in their hands. Then show the cards as fast as you can to the whole group. Give the card to the student who can say the word first. Repeat this a few times at a fast pace.

###  Potato Song Time

Play Track 58 on the CD and sing the song with the students while doing the movements. Display the Story Sentence picture cards so that the students can see them clearly. Sing the song again while pointing at the cards. As an option, students can take turns singing different lines of the song.

**QUICK TIP!** The last page of "At the Beach" shows all eight Memoricons. Students can point to them as they sing.

## Potato Games

### Game 1: Puffing Potatoes

**Players:** 1–16
**Skills:** Fluency
**Age:** 4 and up
**Home use:** no
**Time:** 5–15 minutes
**You need:** Scissors, paper, picture cards 107–114

Show students the Story Sentence cards. Have each student take a piece of paper and draw a fish or other sea creature, then cut it out. It should be about the size of a CD. Make a starting line on the floor and a "goal" such as a desk or a chair (anything will do!). Have all the students line up behind the starting line and place their fish on the floor in front of them. The object of the game is for students to move their fish from the starting line to the goal by blowing it along the floor.

Show students a card that you want to practice. The first student to tell you the word may give their fish one blow. The student to reach the goal first is the winner.

> **NOTE:** Challenge stronger students by having them start farther away from the goal.

### Game 2: Potatomime

**Players:** 4–16
**Skills:** Miming, Story Sentences
**Home use:** Yes
**Time:** 5–15 minutes
**Age:** 5 and up
**You need:** Picture cards 107–114

Divide the students into two teams. Show and say the Story Sentence picture cards. Show a card to a student without the other students seeing it. The student mimes the sentence. The first team to call out the sentence gets a point. Choose another student to mime the next sentence. Gradually reduce the time limit after each round. Play until one team has reached a certain number of points.

> **NOTE:** Some students will be shy about miming. Make it easy for them by doing the mimes with them until they are comfortable.

### Game 3: Nina Says

**Players:** 2–20
**Skills:** Physical response, miming
**Age:** 5 and up
**Home use:** Yes
**Time:** 10–15 minutes
**You need:** Picture cards 107–114

Students stand in a big circle. Show the Story Sentence cards and repeat the sentences while doing the actions. Explain that you are going to do an action from "At the Beach." Tell the students that they must do the action, but only if you say *Nina says* before it. If you don't say *Nina says*, they should do nothing. If they make a mistake and make a move when you haven't said *Nina says*, they must sit down. Play until only one student is standing.

> **NOTE:** For small groups, students can have more than one "out." For more advanced students, you can use different movements for the Story Sentences to make the game more difficult.

**More Practice**

Pages 21–22 in the *Activity Book* and *Workbook* can be used with this lesson. The pages can be done in the classroom or as homework. Please check the answer key on page 90 for *Activity Book* and page 91 for *Workbook*.

# LESSON D2 Focus Words

1. sunglasses
2. sea
3. island
4. dolphin
5. sand castle
6. crab
7. net
8. seal
9. beach ball
10. whale
11. anchor
12. octopus
13. shark
14. shells
15. sandwich
16. peach
17. basket

## Potato Story Time

### Prediction

Ask your students to tell you some of the things they might see at the beach or on the seashore. Think about objects as well as creatures and natural things.

### Reading

After you read each sentence in "At the Beach," point out the Focus Words listed below and ask students to repeat the words.

| |
|---|
| We put on sun block: **sunglasses, sea, island** |
| We play in the sea: **dolphin** |
| We build sand castles: **sand castle** |
| We chase crabs: **crab, net, seal** |
| We swim: **beach ball** |
| We go for a boat ride: **whale, anchor, octopus, shark** |
| We find shells: **shells** |
| We have a picnic: **sandwich, peach, basket** |

**OPTION:** There are other words in the pictures that you can also teach to extend the lesson. Some of these words appear as Focus Words for other books in Book Set 2.

| |
|---|
| We put on sun block: **sun block, sandals, sun, beach umbrella, towel, flower, seagull, beach blanket, coconut tree** |
| We play in the sea: **wave, sea, surfboard, kayak, sailboat** |
| We build sand castles: **bucket, shells, kite, shovel** |
| We chase crabs: **rocks, sea** |
| We swim: **fish, goggles, seahorse, seaweed** |
| We go for a boat ride: **boat, shrimp, sailor, cap** |
| We find shells: **lighthouse, turtle** |
| We have a picnic: **drink, beach blanket, doughnut, ship, chicken** |

## Potato Activities

### Activity 1

Show the Focus Word picture cards, saying the words and clearly repeating them with the students. When the students are confident enough, you can ask one of them to "be the teacher"! That student then shows the cards and leads the class.

**NOTE:** You can use Reading 3 (Tracks 49–57) on the CD. Students will have fun finding the pictures of the words in the "Point and Say" practice.

### Activity 2

Shuffle the Focus Word picture cards. Hold the cards facing away from the students so they cannot see them. Ask students to guess the next card. If they can guess it, give them the card. Continue in this way until all the cards are gone. Ask the students to give the cards back to you as they say what is on them.

**NOTE:** You may want to limit the number of Focus Word cards in this activity to ten or fewer.

# 🎵 Potato Song Time

Play Track 58 on the CD and sing the song with the students while doing the movements. Display the Story Sentence picture cards so that the students can see them clearly. Sing the song again while pointing at the cards. As an option, students can take turns singing different lines of the song.

# 🎲 Potato Games

## Game 1: Potato Fishing

**Players:** 2 or more   **Home use:** Yes
**Skills:** Focus Words   **Time:** 10 minutes
**Age:** 5 and up   **You need:** Picture cards 115–131

Attach metal paper clips to the Focus Word picture cards. Put the cards in a "river" between two rows of students or a "pond" inside a circle of students. Make some simple fishing rods and attach magnets to the end of a piece of string. Students catch the "fish," and if they can say the word, they keep the card. As an alternative, you can ask them to "catch" a word that you say.

## Game 2: Potato Binoculars

**Players:** 2 or more
**Skills:** Focus Words, memory
**Age:** 3 and up
**Home use:** Yes
**Time:** 5–10 minutes
**You need:** Binoculars made out of 2 cardboard rolls

Show, say, and repeat the Focus Words. Position them in various places around the room. Make a pair of binoculars out of two cardboard rolls. Give the binoculars to a student who looks through them at a picture card and says *I can see a (sand castle)*. The next student takes the binoculars and says *I can see a (sand castle) and (shells)*. Continue until someone can't remember the sequence, then start again.

## Game 3: Potato Draw and Pass

**Players:** 2 or more
**Skills:** Focus Words, drawing
**Age:** 6 and up
**Home use:** Yes
**Time:** 10–15 minutes
**You need:** Picture cards 115–131, pencils, paper

Give students pieces of paper and pencils or crayons. Give each student one of the Focus Word cards and ask them to draw a part of what is on the card. They then pass the partially drawn picture to another student who has to draw the rest of the picture and pass it back to the first student, saying what the object was. If the second student is correct, he/she gets a point.

**NOTE:** It is fun to make a display of funny pictures at the end of the game.

### More Practice ✏️

**Pages 23–24 in the *Activity Book* and *Workbook* can be used with this lesson. The pages can be done in the classroom or as homework. Please check the answer key on page 90 for *Activity Book* and page 91 for *Workbook*.**

# LESSON D3 — Topic Words

**Adjectives:**

| | |
|---|---|
| 1. far | 5. light |
| 2. near | 6. heavy |
| 3. long | 7. full |
| 4. short | 8. empty |

##  Potato Story Time

### Prediction

Ask students to tell you any adjectives they know. Prompt them by miming and asking *What's a ~ like?* (of various objects that they know). Draw some groups of objects on the board.

### Reading

After you read the sentence on each page of "At the Beach," point and ask *What's the ~ like?* Help the students with the answers and repeat together.

1. *It's far.* (island)
2. *It's near.* (dolphin)
3. *It's long.* (shovel)
4. *It's short.* (net)
5. *It's light.* (beach ball)
6. *It's heavy.* (anchor)
7. *It's full.* (bucket)
8. *It's empty.* (basket)

## Potato Activities

### Activity 1

Show the students the Topic Word cards and repeat the words. Now shuffle the cards. Pick a card and slowly reveal it to the students bit by bit. As soon as a student

recognizes what it is, he/she may call out the word. When students have said all of the words, shuffle and play again!

**NOTE:** For variety, you can play this game in teams.

### Activity 2

Start a word network like this on the board.

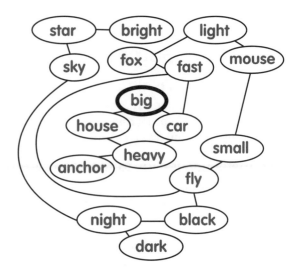

See how far you can expand the network and remember that objects can be described in more than one way. For example, a shovel can be long and heavy.

**NOTE:** Younger pre-reading students may need pictures as well as the words.

## Potato Song Time

Play Track 58 on the CD and sing the song with the students while doing the movements. Display the Story Sentence picture cards so that the students can see them clearly. Sing the song again while pointing at the cards. As an option, students can take turns singing different lines of the song.

**QUICK TIP!** Sometimes you can practice new words by using different words in the same song. Try singing the "At the Beach" song using the Topic Words (adjectives) in the lyrics. Example: *We swim far/We go for a long boat ride*, etc.

## Potato Games

### Game 1: Potato Fishing Trip

**Players:** 2 or more
**Skills:** Remembering adjectives
**Age:** 3 and up
**Home use:** Yes
**Time:** 5–10 minutes
**You need:** Small pieces of paper shaped like fish, picture cards 132–139

Explain to the students that they are going to go on a fishing trip. They will catch a lot of fish if they can say the Topic Words. Practice once by saying and repeating the words with them. Then make a "boat course" around an "island" (a large table or group of chairs). Sit at one point (the "lighthouse") and show children the Topic Word cards as they go past you in their "boats." If they can say the word on the card, give them a fish and repeat the word. If they can't, tell them the word again. The students move around the island catching as many fish as they can.

### Game 2: Potato and Spoon Race

**Players:** Teams of 4–8
**Skills:** Vocabulary, balance
**Age:** 4 and up
**Home use:** Yes
**Time:** 5–15 minutes
**You need:** Picture cards 132–139, potatoes (or balls), spoons

Make teams of not more than eight students per team. Draw or tape a starting line on the floor. The teams line up behind the starting line. Give the student at the front of each line a big spoon and a small potato (or table tennis ball). Have the students place the potatoes in their spoons. You sit in a chair on the opposite side of the room.

The object of the game is for students to reach you without dropping the potato. If the potato drops, they must go back and start again. Show each student who reaches you a card. The student must say the word on the card. Teams get one point for every correct answer.

This is a relay race, so when the students get back to their teams, they give the spoon and potato to the next player. The first team to do a complete round wins.

### Game 3: Potato Lines

**Players:** 6 or more    **Home use:** Yes
**Skills:** Vocabulary    **Time:** 5–15 minutes
**Age:** 3 and up    **You need:** Picture cards

Make two or more lines of students and show a Topic Word card to the first student in line. The student who says the card first runs to the back of his/her line. The other students stay at the front of their lines. The first team to do a complete "round" of all its students is the winner.

**QUICK TIP!** If a student loses three times, give the student a free walk to the back of the line. This will keep the game moving and avoid putting too much pressure on the students who are not as quick.

### More Practice

**Pages 25–26 in the *Activity Book* and *Workbook* can be used with this lesson. The pages can be done in the classroom or as homework. Please check the answer key on page 90 for *Activity Book* and page 91 for *Workbook*.**

# Review

 ## Potato Story Time

### Prediction

Prompt your students to say the Story Sentences from the book by doing the actions from page 48. Ask them to tell you any Focus Words that they can remember. Elicit some of the Topic Words.

### Reading

Encourage your students to read the sentences themselves. Point out Focus Words. Ask *What's the ~ like?* on each page. Be sure to review all of the Topic Words (adjectives).

## ⏰ Potato Activities

### Activity 1

Put the eight Story Sentence cards, eight of the Focus Word cards, and the eight Topic Word (adjective) cards on the floor. Students take turns turning over a card and saying what is on the card. Students try to turn over two of the same type of card—for example, two Focus Word cards. If they do, then they can keep the pair. If the cards are of a different type, they must be turned back over and it is the next student's turn. Make sure all the students say the words

and sentences on the cards as much as possible. Continue until all the cards are off of the floor.

### Activity 2

Make a giant sea poster out of any materials available. Include sea creatures and pictures of potatoes in and out of the water. They can do things from the reader and any other things that students can think of! Remember to have students talk about what they are doing. Sing the "At the Beach" song and have fun!

**NOTE:** This kind of group art project is a wonderful way to develop class friendships and cooperation. It allows students to use English in context both to describe the poster (*What a beautiful fish!*) and to do the task (*Pass the glue, please./Thank you*).

## 🎵 Potato Song Time

Play Track 58 on the CD and sing the song with the students while doing the movements. Display the Story Sentence picture cards so that the students can see them clearly. Sing the song again while pointing at the cards. As an option, students can take turns singing different lines of the song. If you made up a new song in Lesson D3, you can also sing that song.

## 🎲 Potato Games

### Game 1: Potato Grab

**Players:** 2–8    **Home use:** Yes
**Skills:** Vocabulary    **Time:** 5–15 minutes
**Age:** 3 and up    **You need:** Picture cards 107–139

Arrange the Story Sentences, Focus Word, or Topic Word cards faceup in a "pool" either on the floor or on a table. Students stand around the "pool." Say a word. The first student to touch the card with the word can keep it. The student with the most cards at the end of the game is the winner.

You can vary this game by asking your students to start with their hands on their heads or behind their backs, or have them face the other way.

**NOTE:** Make sure that the bigger students do not control the game. Call out some cards that are closer to smaller students.

## Game 2: Potato Footsteps

**Players:** 2–16          **Home use:** Yes
**Skills:** Fluency        **Time:** 5–10 minutes
**Age:** 5 and up          **You need:** A fairly large space

Make a line of students against one wall of the room. Stand at the other end of the room, facing the students. Turn around, face the wall, and slowly say *At the beach, we put on sun block.* Students must try to get to you without being seen to move. They can only move when your back is turned. After you say the sentence, quickly turn around. If you catch any students still moving, they must go back to the wall. The first student who makes it all the way to the front becomes the next caller. Change the sentence each time there is a new round.

**NOTE:** Teach your students to say *You moved!* or *Go back to the wall, please!*

## Game 3: Potato Slap Clap

**Players:** 1–20          **Home use:** Yes
**Skills:** Fluency        **Time:** 5–10 minutes
**Age:** 4 and up          **You need:** Picture cards 107–139

Put the Topic Word cards on the board. Stand in a circle with students and model the following chant:

*Slap, slap, clap, clap,* **far, far**
*Slap, slap, clap, clap,* **near, near**
*Slap, slap, clap, clap,* **long, long**
*Slap, slap, clap, clap,* **short, short**
*Slap, slap, clap, clap,* **light, light**
*Slap, slap, clap, clap,* **heavy, heavy**
*Slap, slap, clap, clap,* **full, full**
*Slap, slap, clap, clap,* **empty, empty**

As you say *slap*, slap your hands on your knees. As you say *clap*, clap your hands.

Do the chant again, but this time go around the circle with a different student saying the adjective each time. Students have to keep the rhythm, but they cannot say the same adjective as the student before them. If they can't say something in time, they are out of that round.

You can vary this game in some of the following ways:

1. Gradually increase the speed of the chant.

2. Replace *Slap, slap, clap, clap* with *What's it like? What's it like? It's~.*

3. Students can't say the same adjective twice in one round.

4. Try your own ideas!

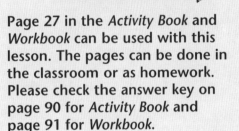

**More Practice**

Page 27 in the *Activity Book* and *Workbook* can be used with this lesson. The pages can be done in the classroom or as homework. Please check the answer key on page 90 for *Activity Book* and page 91 for *Workbook*.

## Draw these things in the picture. Color.

sand castle

crab

whale

shells

octopus

boat

island

seal

# At a Glance

## Book E: At the Zoo

### Story Sentences

At the zoo, we buy tickets.
At the zoo, we learn about animals.
At the zoo, we watch feeding time.
At the zoo, we drink juice.
At the zoo, we pet animals.
At the zoo, we meet our friends.
At the zoo, we eat lunch.
At the zoo, we take pictures.

### Focus Words

| | | | |
|---|---|---|---|
| 1. ticket | 10. kangaroo |
| 2. gorilla | 11. rabbit |
| 3. snake | 12. elephant |
| 4. zebra | 13. bear |
| 5. hippo | 14. tiger |
| 6. crocodile | 15. lion |
| 7. pelican | 16. camera |
| 8. penguin | 17. giraffe |
| 9. koala | 18. monkey |

### Topic Words

Time:

| | |
|---|---|
| 1. 10:00 | 5. 11:00 |
| 2. 10:15 | 6. 11:30 |
| 3. 10:30 | 7. 12:00 |
| 4. 10:45 | 8. 1:00 |

### 🎵 Lyrics

**"At the Zoo"**

At the zoo, we buy tickets
At the zoo, we learn about animals
At the zoo, we watch feeding time
At the zoo, we drink juice

At the zoo, we pet animals
At the zoo, we meet our friends
At the zoo, we eat lunch
At the zoo, we take pictures

*Chorus:*
> At the zoo
> At the zoo
> At the zoo

At the zoo, we buy tickets
At the zoo, we learn about animals
At the zoo, we watch feeding time
At the zoo, we drink juice

At the zoo, we pet animals
At the zoo, we meet our friends
At the zoo, we eat lunch
At the zoo, we take pictures
> *Chorus*

At the zoo!

###  Picture Cards

Use Picture Cards 140–147 (Story Sentences), 148–165 (Focus Words), and 166–173 (Topic Words).

###  CD

Track numbers 59–72 (song is on Track 72)

## LESSON E1 Story Sentences

At the zoo, we buy tickets.
At the zoo, we learn about animals.
At the zoo, we watch feeding time.
At the zoo, we drink juice.
At the zoo, we pet animals.
At the zoo, we meet our friends.
At the zoo, we eat lunch.
At the zoo, we take pictures.

 ## Potato Story Time

### Prediction

Look at the cover of "At the Zoo" together. Explain to the students that this is a story about Buddy's family going to the zoo. Ask them if they have been to a zoo. When did they go? Who did they go with? What did they do there?

### Reading

Read "At the Zoo" or play Tracks 59–60 of the CD. Use the Memoricons (see page 6) and have your students repeat as many of the sentences or parts of the sentences as they can.

**NOTE:** Do not expect too much from this first reading. Your students will probably only be able to repeat bits and pieces. Praise their efforts!

## Potato Activities

### Activity 1

Show the eight Story Sentence picture cards one at a time. Mime the sentences for your students and then do them together:

1. We buy tickets. (Take money from a purse and pay for tickets.)
2. We learn about animals. (Point to an animal book or map.)
3. We watch feeding time. (Pretend to throw fish to a hungry seal.)
4. We drink juice. (Drink from a cup with a straw.)
5. We pet animals. (Pretend to pet an animal.)
6. We meet our friends. (Wave and gesture to some friends.)
7. We eat lunch. (Point to a clock showing 12:00 and pretend to eat.)
8. We take pictures. (Hold a camera and take pictures.)

Now ask individual students to mime phrases and have the other students say what they are doing.

### Activity 2

Make a "zoo" by turning tables into a ticket office and drinks stand, and make animal enclosures with chairs. Choose different students to be "visitors" and "animals." Practice saying the Story Sentences together. Sing the "At the Zoo" song while you are playing.

**NOTE:** This kind of free play can be very creative and a really good way to practice the target language. Don't let things get too wild, though. Remember to have students repeat what you say, and help them to make up their own sentences.

 ## Potato Song Time

Play Track 72 on the CD and sing the song with the students while doing the movements. Display the Story Sentence picture cards so that the students can see them clearly. Sing the song again while pointing at the cards. As an option, students can take turns singing different lines of the song.

> **QUICK TIP!** The last page of "At the Zoo" shows all eight Memoricons. Students can point to them as they sing.

 **Potato Games**

## Game 1: Potato Roll

**Players:** 2–20
**Skills:** Story Sentences, counting
**Age:** 4 and up
**Home use:** Yes
**Time:** 10–15 minutes
**You need:** 2 large homemade dice

Make a die out of recycled materials. You can use milk cartons or something similar. The die should be big enough for all the students to see when it is rolled. Decorate each side of the die with a Story Sentence Memoricon. Students take turns rolling the die and saying the sentences that come up. They get one point for each sentence they can say correctly. Keep score on the board and play to a time limit or up to a certain number of points. This game can be played as a team game.

> **OPTION:** Add a number to each side of the die so that students get different amounts of points for different Story Sentences they can say. Use higher numbers for the sentences that are harder to say.

> **NOTE:** Instead of Memoricons you can put actions (such as *Stand on one leg for a minute*) on the die. This makes the game even more exciting!

## Game 2: Move On!

**Players:** 2–16
**Skills:** Sentence practice
**Age:** 4 and up
**Home use:** Yes
**Time:** 5–10 minutes
**You need:** A picture card from 140–147 for each student

Put the Story Sentence cards in various places around the room where students can see them. As you place the cards, be sure to say, mime, and repeat the phrases. Assign a student to each card. Students take turns saying and miming the sentence on their cards. When you say *Move on!*, students change cards and take turns saying and miming their new sentences.

> **NOTE:** If you have more than one student per card, they can say the sentence together. This is a non-competitive game, but if you want to make it competitive, give students points if they can say the sentences correctly.

## Game 3: Going Home!

**Players:** 2–4 per board
**Skills:** Story Sentences
**Age:** 5 and up
**Home use:** Yes
**Time:** 10–15 minutes
**You need:** Photocopied game board on page 79, a die, some game pieces

Draw the Story Sentence icons in the "houses" on the game board. (For large groups, students can do this themselves if you display the picture cards where they can see them.) Students place their game pieces at START. The youngest player starts and rolls the die. When the student comes to a "house," he/she says the Story Sentence and passes the die to the next player. The first player to reach home is the winner.

> **NOTE:** You can ask higher level students to say all the previous sentences each time they come to a house. You can also make them go back to the previous house if they can't say the sentence.

### More Practice

Pages 28–29 in the *Activity Book* and *Workbook* can be used with this lesson. The pages can be done in the classroom or as homework. Please check the answer key on page 90 for *Activity Book* and page 91 for *Workbook*.

# LESSON E2 — Focus Words

1. ticket
2. gorilla
3. snake
4. zebra
5. hippo
6. crocodile
7. pelican
8. penguin
9. koala
10. kangaroo
11. rabbit
12. elephant
13. bear
14. tiger
15. lion
16. camera
17. giraffe
18. monkey

##  Potato Story Time

### Prediction

Show your students the cover of "At the Zoo," but do not open the book yet. Ask them to remember as many of the sentences or other details from the book as they can. You can ask questions and confirm their answers as you read the book in the next part of the lesson.

### Reading

After you read each sentence in "At the Zoo," point out the Focus Words listed below and ask students to repeat the words.

| We buy tickets: **ticket, gorilla, snake, zebra** |
| --- |
| We learn about animals: **hippo, crocodile** |
| We watch feeding time: **pelican, penguin** |
| We drink juice: **koala, kangaroo** |
| We pet animals: **rabbit** |
| We meet our friends: **elephant** |
| We eat lunch: **bear, tiger, lion** |
| We take pictures: **camera, giraffe, monkey** |

**OPTION:** There are other words in the pictures that you can also teach to extend the lesson. Some of these words appear as Focus Words for other books in Book Set 2.

| We buy tickets: **poster, clock, money, purse** |
| --- |
| We learn about animals: **ostrich, flamingo, map** |
| We watch feeding time: **seal, walrus, fish, zookeeper, bucket** |
| We drink juice: **drinks, polar bear, juice machine, refrigerator** |
| We pet animals: **sheep, goat, ducks, ducklings** |
| We meet our friends: **water, backpack** |
| We eat lunch: **sandwiches, lunch box, juice** |
| We take pictures: **camel** |

## ⏰ Potato Activities

### Activity 1

Show the Focus Word picture cards, saying the words and clearly repeating them with the students. When the students are confident enough, you can ask one of them to "be the teacher"! That student then shows the cards and leads the class.

**NOTE:** You can use Reading 3 (Tracks 63–71) on the CD. Students will have fun finding the pictures of the words in the "Point and Say" practice.

### Activity 2

Show, say, and repeat the Focus Word picture cards. Then, turn one of the cards upside down. Show the cards and have students repeat the words again. When you come to the upside-down card, the students have to stand up and say a sentence from the book. Continue in this way, putting a different card upside down each time.

## 🎵 Potato Song Time

Play Track 72 on the CD and sing the song with the students while doing the movements. Display the Story Sentence picture cards so that the students can see them clearly. Sing the song again while pointing at the cards. As an option, students can take turns singing different lines of the song.

**OPTION:** Make up your own song using the Focus Words in the lyrics. For example: *At the zoo, we see zebras/At the zoo, we learn about gorillas/At the zoo, we watch crocodiles/At the zoo, we see snakes*, etc.

## Potato Games

### Game 1: Potato Skittles

**Players:** 2–16
**Skills:** Focus Words, rolling a ball
**Age:** 4 and up
**Home use:** Yes
**Time:** 10 to make, 15 to play
**You need:** Cardboard tubes or bottles, tennis ball

Make eight skittles (bowling pins) from cardboard paper towel tubes or milk cartons. Decorate them with pictures of some of the animals from "At the Zoo." Divide the class into two or more teams. Select two students to be "umpires." Mark a line on the floor from behind which students will roll the ball. Students take turns rolling the ball and trying to knock over the pins. The umpires replace the pins while showing them to the other students. Keep score by giving one point for each animal knocked over and said aloud. Play to a time limit or until one team has scored a certain number of points.

**NOTES:** Increase the number of pins by adding more animals.

### Game 2: Potato Jigsaws

**Players:** 1 or more   **Home use:** Yes
**Skills:** Vocabulary   **Time:** 5–15 minutes
**Age:** 3 and up   **You need:** Cardboard, scissors

Make simple jigsaw puzzles of the Focus Words you want to practice. Students can make these themselves if they are able to use scissors or you can prepare the puzzles in advance. You can either give each student in the group a piece and have them cooperate to put the puzzle together or give them individual puzzles. You can even have races between teams or groups. Make sure to say the words as much as possible.

**NOTE:** You can vary the level of difficulty depending of the age and ability of your students.

### Game 3: Potato Sack

**Players:** 1–16
**Skills:** Focus Words, throwing
**Age:** 3 and up
**Home use:** Yes
**Time:** 5–15 minutes
**You need:** A beanbag, picture cards 148–165

Put the Focus Word cards you want to practice on the floor in a "pool." Tape a line on the floor or use a rope that students must stand behind. Students stand behind this line and take turns tossing a beanbag into the "pool." If the beanbag lands on a card, the student says the word and takes the card. Continue until all the cards are gone.

**QUICK TIP!** Place the line depending upon the students' age. Make the game more challenging for older students by having them take a step backwards each time they get a card.

## More Practice

Pages 30–31 in the *Activity Book* and *Workbook* can be used with this lesson. The pages can be done in the classroom or as homework. Please check the answer key on page 90 for *Activity Book* and page 92 for *Workbook*.

# Topic Words

**Time:**

1. 10:00 (ten o'clock)
2. 10:15 (ten fifteen)
3. 10:30 (ten thirty)
4. 10:45 (ten forty-five)
5. 11:00 (eleven o'clock)
6. 11:30 (eleven thirty)
7. 12:00 (twelve o'clock)
8. 1:00 (one o'clock)

## Potato Story Time

### Prediction

Ask your students *What time is it now?* Talk about the time. Ask them if they know what time they do certain things during the day (get up, go to school, have a snack, have lunch, etc.). Draw some clocks on the board, saying the times and repeating them with the students.

### Reading

After you read the sentence on each page of "At the Zoo," point to the clock and ask *What time is it?* Help them with the answers and repeat together.

1. *It's ten o'clock.* (10:00)
2. *It's ten fifteen.* (10:15)
3. *It's ten thirty.* (10:30)
4. *It's ten forty-five.* (10:45)
5. *It's eleven o'clock.* (11:00)
6. *It's eleven thirty.* (11:30)
7. *It's twelve o'clock.* (12:00)
8. *It's one o'clock.* (1:00)

## Potato Activities

### Activity 1

Show your students the time cards and ask *What time is it?* after you show each one. Give out a card to each student, saying the time as you hand it out. Then say *(Ten o'clock), please,* and have the students with that card give the card back to you.

Practice the time by asking your students *What time is it?* as you hold up a time card. As soon as possible, encourage your students to ask each other the questions as they point to a page in "At the Zoo."

### Activity 2

Put the Topic Word cards for the time (166–173) in various places around the room. Tell students to move to the correct card as you say the times. When they gather by each card, have them repeat the time. As soon as possible, get a student to be the leader and call out the time words.

**NOTE:** You can make other cards with different times on them as students gain confidence. It can be fun to make these in different shapes and sizes.

## Potato Wisdom

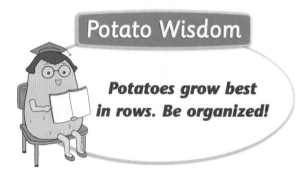

*Potatoes grow best in rows. Be organized!*

## Potato Song Time

Play Track 72 on the CD and sing the song with the students while doing the movements. Display the Story Sentence picture cards so that the students can see them clearly. Sing the song again while pointing at the cards. As an option, students can take turns singing different lines of the song.

## Potato Games

### Game 1: What Time Is It?

**Players:** 2–20     **Home use:** Yes
**Skills:** Topic Words   **Time:** 5–10 minutes
**Age:** 4 and up     **You need:** Picture cards 166–173

Students line up against the wall. You stand at one end of the room facing them. Give each student a number from 1–10. Students say *What time is it?* Say a time and have the students whose number matches the first number in the time phrase move that number of steps towards you. For example, if you say *Two o'clock*, students whose number is two must take two steps towards you. Let the first student who tags you be "it." This student then says the times.

### Game 2: Body Clocks

**Players:** 2–20     **Home use:** Yes
**Skills:** Topic Words   **Time:** 5–10 minutes
**Age:** 6 and up     **You need:** Picture cards 166–173

Show the students the Topic word picture cards, say the times, and repeat with the students. Display the cards somewhere that they can see them. Show them how to make times with their arms as the hands of a clock. Practice making some of the times together with the students. Now shuffle the cards and show cards at random. Students try to make the times. Give points to the fastest student or the team which has all its members making the correct time first.

**NOTE:** You can make this game more challenging by just saying the times and not showing the students the cards.

### Game 3: Potato Mistake

**Players:** 2–20     **Home use:** Yes
**Skills:** Vocabulary   **Time:** 5–10 minutes
**Age:** 4 and up     **You need:** Picture cards 166–173

Students stand up. Show the Topic Word cards as you say each time and have students repeat. Tell students that you will say the words again, but you will make a mistake and say a time that is not on one of the cards. Tell them they can not repeat that time. If they do repeat the incorrect time, they must sit down. Play for a period of time or until there is only one student standing.

## More Practice

Pages 32–33 in the *Activity Book* and *Workbook* can be used with this lesson. The pages can be done in the classroom or as homework. Please check the answer key on page 90 for *Activity Book* and page 92 for *Workbook*.

# Review

## 📖 Potato Story Time

### Prediction

Prompt your students to say the Story Sentences from the book by doing the actions from page 58. Ask them to tell you any Focus Words that they can remember. Elicit some of the Topic Words by drawing clocks on the board.

### Reading

Encourage your students to read the sentences themselves. Point out Focus Words. Ask *What's the time?* on each page. Be sure to review all of the Topic Words for time.

## 🕐 Potato Activities

### Activity 1

Put the eight Story Sentence cards, eight Focus Word cards and the eight Topic Word cards on the floor. Students take turns turning over a card and saying what is on the card. Students try to turn over two of the same type of card—for example, two Focus Word cards. If they do, then they can keep the pair. If the cards are of a different type, they must be turned back over and it is the next student's turn. Make sure all the students say the words and sentences on the cards as much as possible. Continue until all the cards are off of the floor.

### Activity 2

Show the students the Topic Word cards and repeat the words. Now shuffle the cards. Pick a card and slowly reveal it to the students bit by bit. As soon as a student recognizes what it is, he/she may call out the word. When students have said all of the words, shuffle and play again!

## Potato Wisdom

*Young potatoes have thin skins. Treat them with care!*

## 💿🎵 Potato Song Time

Play Track 72 on the CD and sing the song with the students while doing the movements. Display the Story Sentence picture cards so that the students can see them clearly. Sing the song again while pointing at the cards. As an option, students can take turns singing different lines of the song. If you made a new song in E2, you can also sing that song.

 **Potato Games**

## Game 1: Potato!

**Players:** 2 or more
**Skills:** Recognizing vocabulary
**Age:** 3 and up
**Home use:** Yes
**Time:** 15 minutes
**You need:** Photocopied "Potato!" sheets (page 78), picture cards 148–165

Photocopy one "Potato!" sheet for each student. Show the Focus Word picture cards. Say the words and repeat. Fix the cards somewhere the students can see them. Students draw or write the words on their "Potato!" sheets at random. When they have completed their sheets, shuffle the cards and call the words out one at a time. Students circle the words you call out saying *I found it!* As in Bingo, the first student to get a line of potatoes calls out *POTATO!* You can play in vertical, horizontal, or diagonal lines.

## Game 2: Hot Potatoes

**Players:** 2 or more      **Home use:** Yes
**Skills:** Fluency            **Time:** As long as you like!
**Age:** 3 and up             **You need:** Any soft ball, a timer

Set a kitchen timer for one minute or use the classroom clock. Students make a circle and pass a ball around saying *At the zoo, we buy tickets* until the timer goes off. The student holding the ball at that time leaves the circle. Continue, saying a different sentence each time until there is only one student.

**OPTION:** Give students more "outs." For 6–12 students, give each student 3 outs. For over 12 students, give each student 2 outs.

## Game 3: Missing Potatoes

**Players:** 2–20
**Skills:** Memory
**Age:** 5 and up
**Home use:** Yes
**Time:** 3 minutes per round
**You need:** Picture cards 140–147

Attach the Story Sentence picture cards to the board while saying the sentences with your students. Ask your students to face away from the board. Remove a card and hide it behind your back. Students turn around and look at the board. Give the card to the student who can say which card is missing. Continue until all the cards are gone.

 **QUICK TIP!** You can make students "take a rest" for a turn after they answer, allowing other students to catch up. If students can't say the whole phrase, give them hints by saying part of it for them and just have them finish the phrase.

### More Practice

**Pages 34 in the *Activity Book* and *Workbook* can be used with this lesson. The pages can be done in the classroom or as homework. Please check the answer key on page 90 for *Activity Book* and page 92 for *Workbook*.**

# Draw the animals at the zoo.

# At a Glance

## Book F: On the Farm

### Story Sentences

On the farm, we milk cows.
On the farm, we ride horses.
On the farm, we feed pigs.
On the farm, we play with puppies.
On the farm, we collect eggs.
On the farm, we pick berries.
On the farm, we make pies.
On the farm, we have a great time!

### Focus Words

1. cow
2. horse
3. rainbow
4. pig
5. apple
6. stick
7. tractor
8. hen
9. sheep
10. berries
11. duck

### Topic Words

Family:

1. father
2. mother
3. brother
4. sister
5. uncle
6. aunt
7. grandmother
8. grandfather

 **Lyrics**

"On the Farm"

We milk cows
We ride horses
We feed pigs
We play with puppies

We collect eggs
We pick berries
We make pies
We have a great time!

*Chorus:*

On the farm
On the farm
On the farm
On the farm

On the farm
On the farm
On the farm
On the farm

*Repeat all*

 **Picture Cards**

Use Picture Cards 174–181 (Story Sentences), 182–192 (Focus Words), and 193–200 (Topic Words).

**CD**

Track numbers 73–86 (song is on Track 86)

# Story Sentences

On the farm, we milk cows.
On the farm, we ride horses.
On the farm, we feed pigs.
On the farm, we play with puppies.
On the farm, we collect eggs.
On the farm, we pick berries.
On the farm, we make pies.
On the farm, we have a great time!

 ## Potato Story Time

### Prediction

Look at the cover of "On the Farm" together. Explain to the students that this is a story about Joy's visit to her grandparents' farm. Focus students on things that they might see on a farm. Write some of their answers on the board.

### Reading

Read "On the Farm" or play Tracks 73–74 of the CD. Use the Memoricons (see page 6) and have your students repeat as many of the sentences or parts of the sentences as they can.

**NOTE:** Do not expect too much from this first reading. Your students will probably only be able to repeat bits and pieces. Praise their efforts!

## Potato Activities

### Activity 1

Show the eight Story Sentence picture cards one at a time. Mime the sentences for your students and then do them together:

1. We milk cows. (Squeeze and pull down your fists rhythmically.)
2. We ride horses. (Trot along with your hands in front of you as if holding reins.)
3. We feed pigs. (Pretend to pour out a bucket of feed.)
4. We play with puppies. (Throw a stick.)
5. We collect eggs. (Pretend to reach your hand under a chicken.)
6. We pick berries. (Make picking movements.)
7. We make pies. (Carefully take a pie out of an oven. Breathe in the smell of the pie.)
8. We have a great time! (Raise your hands above your head and SMILE!)

Now ask individual students to do the actions and have the other students say what they are doing.

### Activity 2

Show your students the Story Sentence cards and have them repeat the sentences while doing the movements. Tell the students that they are the farmer and that you are a farm worker who will do anything they say. They will enjoy ordering you to do the sentences from the book! When you have done this for a few minutes, put the students into pairs. Make one the farmer and the farm worker.

**NOTE:** Change roles often! No one likes to be told what to do all the time!

 ## Potato Song Time

Play Track 86 on the CD and sing the song with the students while doing the movements. Display the Story Sentence picture cards so that the students can see them clearly. Sing the song again while pointing at the cards. As an option, students can take turns singing different lines of the song.

 **Potato Games**

### Game 1: Roll-a-Potato

**Players:** 4 or more
**Skills:** Story Sentences, rolling a ball
**Age:** 4 and up
**Home use:** Yes
**Time:** 5 minutes
**You need:** Picture cards 174–181, a ball

Students sit in a circle and roll a ball to each other, saying the first Story Sentence, *On the farm, we ride in the car*. When they have practiced enough, show them the next card, *On the farm, we go hiking*. Continue like this until they have said all the cards. Then show cards at random and ask individual students to say the sentences. If they can say the sentence, they can roll the ball. If they can't, they must give the ball to the student on their left and skip a turn.

> **NOTE:** Help less advanced students so that everyone has a chance to roll the ball. You can make the activity more challenging by putting some empty plastic bottles in the middle of the circle. Students must not knock over the bottles as they roll the ball.

### Game 2: Potatomime

**Players:** 4–16
**Skills:** Miming, sentence practice
**Age:** 5 and up
**Home use:** Yes
**Time:** 5–15 minutes
**You need:** Picture cards 174–181

Divide the students into two teams. Show and say the Story Sentence picture cards (174–181). Show a student a card without the other students seeing it. The student mimes the sentence. The first team to call out the sentence gets a point. Choose another student to mime the next sentence. Gradually reduce the time limit after each round. Play until one team has reached a certain number of points.

> **NOTE:** Some students will be shy about miming. Make it easy for them by doing the mimes with them until they are comfortable.

### Game 3: Potato Footsteps

**Players:** 2–16
**Skills:** Fluency
**Age:** 5 and up
**Home use:** Yes
**Time:** 5–10 minutes
**You need:** A fairly large space

Make a line of students against one wall of the room. Stand at the other end of the room, facing the students. Turn around, face the wall, and slowly say *On the farm, we milk cows*. Students must try to get to you without being seen to move. They can only move when your back is turned. After you say the sentence, quickly turn around. If you catch any students still moving, they must go back to the wall. The first student who makes it all the way to the front becomes the next caller. Change the sentence each time there is a new round.

> **NOTE:** Teach your students to say *You moved!* or *Go back to the wall, please!*

**More Practice**

**Pages 35–36 in the *Activity Book* and *Workbook* can be used with this lesson. The pages can be done in the classroom or as homework. Please check the answer key on page 90 for *Activity Book* and page 92 for *Workbook*.**

## LESSON F2 — Focus Words

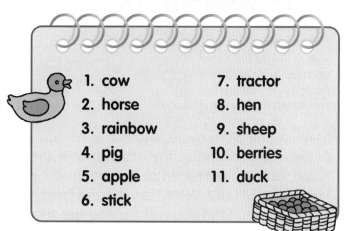

1. cow
2. horse
3. rainbow
4. pig
5. apple
6. stick
7. tractor
8. hen
9. sheep
10. berries
11. duck

**OPTION:** There are other words in the pictures that you can also teach to extend the lesson. Some of these words appear as Focus Words for other books in Book Set 2.

| | |
|---|---|
| We milk cows: | **bucket, milk, flies, cap, stool, straw** |
| We ride horses: | **barn, riding hat, reins, saddle** |
| We feed pigs: | **bucket, carrots, boots, fence** |
| We play with puppies: | **farm house, tree** |
| We collect eggs: | **nest, hen house** |
| We pick berries: | **basket, bush** |
| We make pies: | **glasses, cat, refrigerator, table, pie, oven mitts, rolling pin, mixing bowl, flour, berries** |
| We have a great time!: | **knife, pond, fence, dishes, pie, table** |

 ## Potato Story Time

### Prediction

Show your students the cover of "On the Farm," but do not open the book yet. Ask them to remember any of the objects or animals they saw in the book. Help them by doing the movements for each sentence. Write the names and draw simple pictures of the objects they say on the board, even if the objects do not appear in the story.

### Reading

After you read each sentence in "On the Farm," point out the Focus Words listed below and ask students to repeat the words.

| | |
|---|---|
| We milk cows: | **cow** |
| We ride horses: | **horse, rainbow** |
| We feed pigs: | **pig, apple** |
| We play with puppies: | **stick, tractor** |
| We collect eggs: | **hen** |
| We pick berries: | **sheep** |
| We make pies: | **berries** |
| We have a great time!: | **duck** |

## Potato Activities

### Activity 1

Show the Focus Word picture cards, saying the words and clearly repeating them with the students. When the students are confident enough, you can ask one of them to "be the teacher"! That student then shows the cards and leads the class.

**NOTE:** You can use Reading 3 (Tracks 77–85) on the CD. Students will have fun finding the pictures of the words in the "Point and Say" practice.

### Activity 2

Shuffle the Focus Word picture cards. Hold the cards facing away from the students so they cannot see them. Ask students to guess the next card. If they can guess it, give them the card. Continue in this way until all the cards are gone. Ask the students to give the cards back to you as they say what is on them.

**NOTE:** You may want to limit the number of Focus Word cards in this activity to ten or fewer.

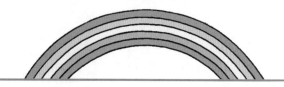

# 🎵 Potato Song Time

Play Track 86 on the CD and sing the song with the students while doing the movements. Display the Story Sentence picture cards so that the students can see them clearly. Sing the song again while pointing at the cards. As an option, students can take turns singing different lines of the song.

# ♟ Potato Games

## Game 1: Potato Grab

**Players:** 2–8          **Home use:** Yes
**Skills:** Vocabulary    **Time:** 5–15 minutes
**Age:** 3 and up         **You need:** Picture cards 182–192

Arrange the Focus Word cards faceup in a "pool" either on the floor or on a table. Students stand around the "pool." Say a word. The first student to touch the card with the word can keep it. The student with the most cards at the end of the game is the winner.

You can vary this game by asking your students to start with their hands on their heads or behind their backs, or have them face the other way.

**NOTE:** Make sure that the bigger students do not control the game. Call out some cards that are closer to smaller students.

## Game 2: Potato Draw and Pass

**Players:** 2 or more
**Skills:** Focus Words, drawing
**Age:** 6 and over
**Home use:** Yes
**Time:** 10–15 minutes
**You need:** Picture cards 182–192, pencils, paper

Give students pieces of paper and pencils or crayons. Give each student one of the Focus Word cards and ask them to draw a part of what is on the card. They then pass the partially drawn picture to another student who has to draw the rest of the picture and pass it back to the first student, saying what the object was. If the second student is correct, he/she gets a point.

**NOTE:** It is fun to have an exhibition of funny pictures at the end of the game.

## Game 3: Potato Lines

**Players:** 2–8          **Home use:** Yes
**Skills:** Vocabulary    **Time:** 5–15 minutes
**Age:** 3 and up         **You need:** Picture cards 182–192

Make two or more lines of students and show a Focus Word card to the first student in line. The student who says the card first runs to the back of his/her line. The other students stay at the front of their lines. The first team to do a complete "round" of all its students is the winner.

**QUICK TIP!** If a student loses three times, give the student a free walk to the back of the line. This will keep the game moving and avoid putting too much pressure on the students who are not as quick.

## More Practice

Pages 37–38 in the *Activity Book* and *Workbook* can be used with this lesson. The pages can be done in the classroom or as homework. Please check the answer key on page 90 for *Activity Book* and page 92 for *Workbook*.

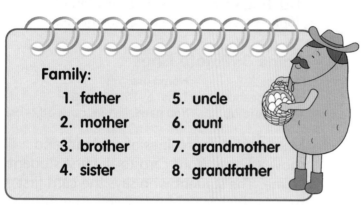

## LESSON F3 Topic Words

**Family:**
1. father
2. mother
3. brother
4. sister
5. uncle
6. aunt
7. grandmother
8. grandfather

##  Potato Story Time

### Prediction

Ask your students how many people there are in their families. Talk about the words for family members. Draw a family tree on the board.

### Reading

After you read the sentence on each page of "On the Farm," point and ask *Who is with Joy?* Help students with the answers and repeat together.

1. *It's her father.*
2. *It's her mother.*
3. *It's her brother.*
4. *It's her sister.*
5. *It's her uncle.*
6. *It's her aunt.*
7. *It's her grandmother.*
8. *It's her grandfather.*

## Potato Activities

### Activity 1

Show your students the Topic Word cards for family members (193–200) and ask *Who is this?* after you show each one. Give out a card to each student, saying the family word as you hand it out. Then say *(Father), please,* and have the students with that card give it back to you.

### Activity 2

Put the Topic Word cards for family members (193–200) in various places around the room. Tell students to move to the correct card as you say each word. When they gather by the card, have them repeat the word. As soon as possible, get a student to be the leader and call out the family members.

**NOTE:** For larger, seated classes, students can just point to the cards.

##  Potato Song Time

Play Track 86 on the CD and sing the song with the students while doing the movements. Display the Story Sentence picture cards so that the students can see them clearly. Sing the song again while pointing at the cards. As an option, students can take turns singing different lines of the song.

> **QUICK TIP!** Sometimes you can practice new words using different words in the same song. Try singing the "On the Farm" song using the Topic Words (family) in the lyrics.

## Potato Games

### Game 1: Happy Families

**Players:** 3 or more players in groups of less than 5
**Skills:** Topic Words
**Age:** 5 and up
**Home use:** Yes
**Time:** 10–15 minutes
**You need:** Photocopiable "Happy Families" cards from page 81

Make the cards in advance. Show, say, and repeat the cards to the students. Shuffle the cards and deal them out to the players. Players take turns drawing a card from the player next to them. Players then put down pairs of cards from the same family. The first person to put down all their cards is the winner.

## Potato Wisdom

*Good potatoes go well with everything. Good teachers get along with everyone!*

## Game 2: Potato Slap Clap

**Players:** 1–20
**Skills:** Fluency
**Age:** 4 and up
**Home use:** Yes
**Time:** 5–10 minutes
**You need:** Picture cards 193–200

Put the Topic Word cards on the board. Stand in a circle with students and model the following chant:

*Slap, slap, clap, clap,* **father, father**

*Slap, slap, clap, clap,* **mother, mother**

*Slap, slap, clap, clap,* **brother, brother**

*Slap, slap, clap, clap,* **sister, sister**

*Slap, slap, clap, clap,* **uncle, uncle**

*Slap, slap, clap, clap,* **aunt, aunt**

*Slap, slap, clap, clap,* **grandmother, grandmother**

*Slap, slap, clap, clap,* **grandfather, grandfather**

As you say *slap,* slap your hands on your knees. As you say *clap,* clap your hands.

Do the chant again, but this time go around the circle with a different student saying the feeling each time. Students have to keep the rhythm but cannot say the same family member as the student before them. If they can't say something in time, they are out of that round.

**NOTE:** You can vary this game in some of the following ways:

1. Gradually increase the speed of the chant.

2. Replace *Slap, slap, clap, clap* with *Who's that? Who's that? It's ~.*

3. Say that students can't say the same family member twice in one round.

4. Try your own ideas!

## Game 3: Missing Potatoes

**Players:** 2–20
**Skills:** Memory
**Age:** 5 and up
**Home use:** Yes
**Time:** 3 minutes per round
**You need:** Picture cards 193–200

Attach the Topic Word picture cards to the board while saying the words with your students. Ask your students to face away from the board. Remove a card and hide it behind your back. Students turn around and look at the board. Give the card to the student who can say which card is missing. Continue until all the cards are gone.

**QUICK TIP!** You can make students "take a rest" for a turn after they answer, allowing other students to catch up. If students can't say the word, give them hints.

## More Practice

Pages 39–40 in the *Activity Book* and *Workbook* can be used with this lesson. The pages can be done in the classroom or as homework. Please check the answer key on page 90 for *Activity Book* and page 92 for *Workbook.*

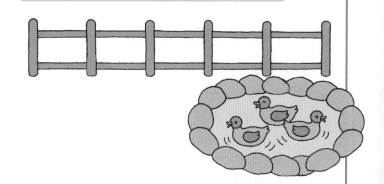

**Potato Story Time**

### Prediction

Prompt your students to say the Story Sentences from the book by doing the actions from page 68. Ask them to tell you any Focus Words that they can remember. Elicit some of the Topic Words by drawing a family tree on the board.

### Reading

Encourage your students to read the sentences themselves. Point out Focus Words. Ask *Who is with Joy?* on each page. Be sure to review all of the Topic Words for family members.

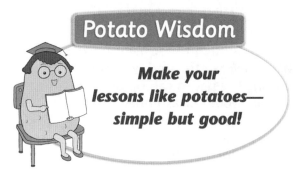

Potato Wisdom

*Make your lessons like potatoes— simple but good!*

### Potato Activities

### Activity 1

Make a family tree poster either of:

1. Students' real families

   Students bring in photos of their families or draw pictures that you attach to a large piece of paper.

2. Imaginary families

   This could be a family of people cut from magazines and stuck to the paper.

### Activity 2

Show the students the Focus Word cards and repeat the words. Now shuffle the cards. Pick a card and slowly reveal it to the students bit by bit. As soon as a student recognizes what it is, he/she may call out the word. When students have said all of the words, shuffle and play again!

### Potato Song Time

Play Track 86 on the CD and sing the song with the students while doing the movements. Display the Story Sentence picture cards so that the students can see them clearly. Sing the song again while pointing at the cards. As an option, students can take turns singing different lines of the song. If you made up a new song in Lesson F3, you can also sing that song.

### Potato Games

### Game 1: Arrows!

**Players:** 2–4 per board
**Skills:** Reviewing all Book F language
**Age:** 5 and over
**Home use:** Yes
**Time:** 10–20 minutes
**You need:** Photocopies of the "Arrows!" game board on page 80, a die, game pieces

Copy the Focus Words, Topic Words and Story Sentence picture cards that you want to practice into some of the blank spaces on the game board. You don't need to fill them all.

Players put their game pieces on START. The youngest player rolls the die and moves his/her game piece that number of spaces. If the student lands directly on an arrow space, he/she must follow the direction of that arrow on the next turn. If the student lands on a word or sentence space and can say the word or sentence, he/she may roll the die again.

**NOTE:** Students might enjoy decorating the game board with items from the book. You can modify this game board to practice the language from any of the readers.

## Game 2: Mashed Potatoes

**Players:** 2–12
**Skills:** Remembering Book F language
**Age:** 4 and up
**Home use:** Yes
**Time:** 5–10 minutes
**ou need:** Picture cards 174–200

Place the cards you want to practice faceup on the floor where all the students can see them. Secretly write one of the words or sentences on a piece of paper. Students take turns saying the words or sentences. When the word is said, the card is turned over. If a student chooses the word or sentence you have secretly written, he/she is "mashed" (out of the game). Each time this happens you turn all the cards faceup again and choose another word (it can be the same word!). Continue until only one student remains unmashed!

## Game 3: Hot Potatoes

**Players:** 2 and up
**Skills:** Fluency
**Age:** 3 and up
**Home use:** Yes
**Time:** As long as you like!
**You need:** Any soft ball, timer

Set a kitchen timer for one minute or use the classroom clock. Students make a circle and pass a ball around saying *On the farm, we milk cows* until the timer goes off. The student holding the ball at that time leaves the circle. Continue, saying a different sentence each time until there is only one student.

**OPTION:** Give students more "outs." For 6–12 students, give each student 3 outs. For over 12 students, give each student 2 outs.

### More Practice

Page 41 in the *Activity Book* and *Workbook* can be used with this lesson. The pages can be done in the classroom or as homework. Please check the answer key on page 90 for *Activity Book* and page 92 for *Workbook*.

## Cut, stick, and color.

# Potato Pals Theme Song

A good way to warm up your students is to begin every lesson by singing the "Potato Pals Theme Song." Play Track 2 of the CD. You can make copies of the lyric sheet below if you want students to follow along, or you can use it as your own reference for the lyrics.

One, two, three four!
Four, three, two, one!

One potato
Two potatoes
Three potatoes
Four potatoes
Five potatoes
Six Potato Pals!

Buddy!
Daisy!
Chip!
Dean!
Nina!
Joy!
Your Potato Pals!

One potato
Two potatoes
Three potatoes
Four potatoes
Five potatoes
Six Potato Pals!

Buddy!
Daisy!
Chip!
Dean!
Nina!
Joy!
Your Potato Pals!

One potato
Two potatoes
Three potatoes
Four potatoes
Five potatoes
Six Potato Pals!

Everybody loves potatoes
Everybody loves potatoes
Everybody loves Potato Pals!

Everybody loves potatoes
Everybody loves potatoes
Everybody loves Potato Pals!

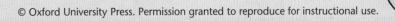

# Potato!

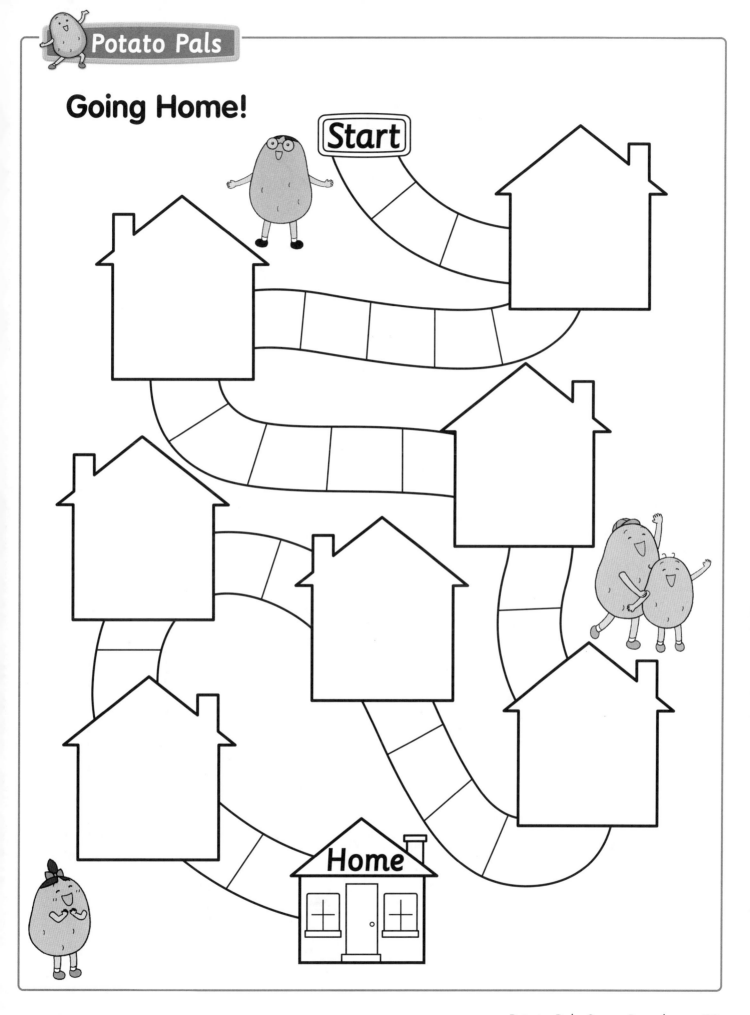

# Potato Pals

## Going Home!

Start

Home

Potato Pals Game Boards

# Arrows!

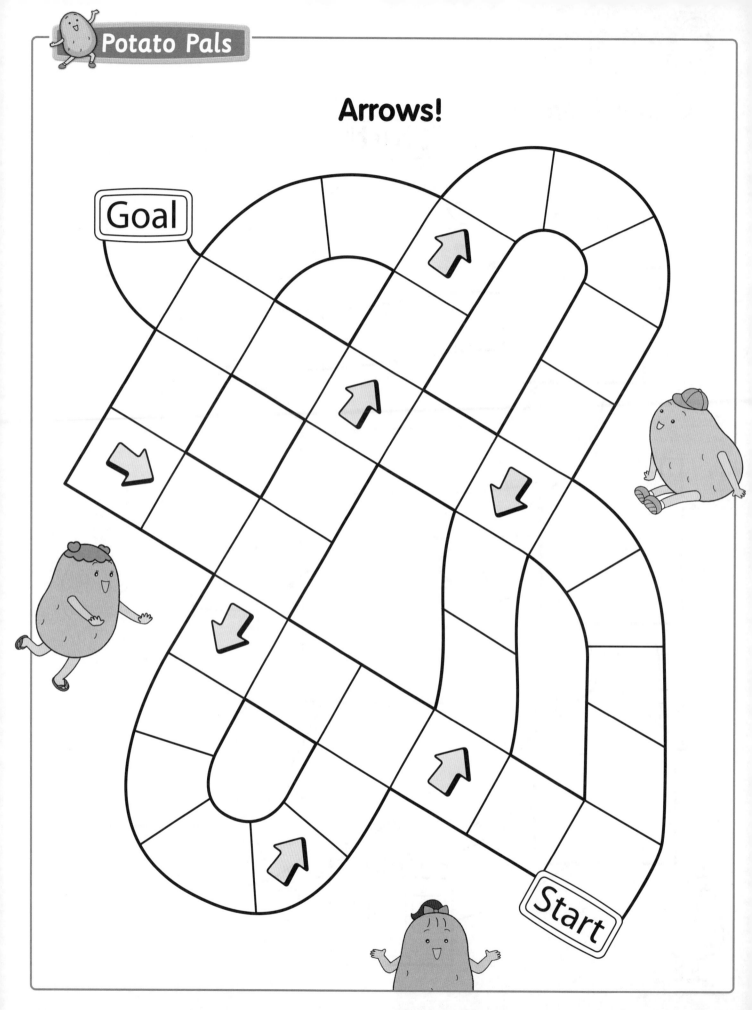

Goal

Start

# Happy Families

Dean | Dean's mother | Dean's father | Dean's sister

Joy | Joy's grandfather | Joy's grandmother | Joy's brother

Nina | Nina's father | Nina's mother | Nina's aunt

Buddy | Buddy's father | Buddy's mother | Buddy's brother

# Point and Say Audio Script

This section of the User's Guide goes with Reading 3 on the CD for each book. You can refer to this section when you use the CD with your students or you can use it for review later without the CD. The track is listed first, followed by the language that is heard on the track.

**Track 8:**
**A:** At the store, we find a cart.
**B:** Can you find these things? Point and say.
**C:** bicycle • cart
**B:** What can the baby do?
**A:** She can push.

**Track 9:**
**A:** At the store, we go inside.
**B:** Can you find these things? Point and say.
**C:** onion • carrots • cabbage
**B:** What can the baby do?
**A:** She can pull.

**Track 10:**
**A:** At the store, we look for things.
**B:** Can you find these things? Point and say.
**C:** bananas • orange • grapes
**B:** What can the baby do?
**A:** She can point.

**Track 11:**
**A:** At the store, we fill the cart.
**B:** Can you find these things? Point and say.
**C:** bread • milk • cereal
**B:** What can the baby do?
**A:** She can shake.

**Track 12:**
**A:** At the store, we wait in line.
**B:** Can you find these things? Point and say.
**C:** tomato • cookies • melon
**B:** What can the baby do?
**A:** She can throw.

**Track 13:**
**A:** At the store, we pay.
**B:** Can you find these things? Point and say.
**C:** money • cheese
**B:** What can the baby do?
**A:** She can catch.

**Track 14:**
**A:** At the store, we put things in bags.
**B:** Can you find these things? Point and say.
**C:** chocolate • lemon
**B:** What can the baby do?
**A:** She can clap.

**Track 15:**
**A:** At the store, we load the car.
**B:** Can you find these things? Point and say.
**C:** watermelon • motorcycle
**B:** What can the baby do?
**A:** She can carry.

**Track 22:**
**A:** On a camping trip, we ride in the car.
**B:** Can you find these things? Point and say.
**C:** leaves • mountain
**B:** Look at the car. What's it like?
**A:** It's fast.

**Track 23:**
**A:** On a camping trip, we go hiking.
**B:** Can you find these things? Point and say.
**C:** backpack • turtle
**B:** Look at the turtle. What's it like?
**A:** It's slow.

**Track 24:**
**A:** On a camping trip, we put up our tent.
**B:** Can you find these things? Point and say.
**C:** tent • mountain
**B:** Look at the tent. What's it like?
**A:** It's new.

**Track 25:**
**A:** On a camping trip, we go fishing.
**B:** Can you find these things? Point and say.
**C:** fish • river • fishing rod
**B:** Look at the boot. What's it like?
**A:** It's old.

**Track 26:**
**A:** On a camping trip, we have a barbecue.
**B:** Can you find these things? Point and say.
**C:** salad • chicken • corn • hot dog
**B:** Look at the corn. What's it like?
**A:** It's big.

**Track 27:**
**A:** On a camping trip, we sing songs.
**B:** Can you find these things? Point and say.
**C:** guitar • squirrel • fire
**B:** Look at the guitar. What's it like?
**A:** It's small.

**Track 28:**
**A:** On a camping trip, we count the stars.
**B:** Can you find these things? Point and say.
**C:** owl • fox • star
**B:** Look at the shooting star. What's it like?
**A:** It's bright.

**Track 29:**
**A:** On a camping trip, we say "Good night!"
**B:** Can you find these things? Point and say.
**C:** flashlight • sky
**B:** Look at the sky. What's it like?
**A:** It's dark.

**Track 36:**
**A:** In town, we buy candy.
**B:** Can you find these things? Point and say.
**C:** candy • balloon
**B:** Find the vehicle. What is it?
**A:** It's a train.

**Track 37:**
**A:** In town, we get haircuts.
**B:** Can you find these things? Point and say.
**C:** barber shop
**B:** Find the vehicle. What is it?
**A:** It's an ambulance.

**Track 38:**
**A:** In town, we mail letters.
**B:** Can you find these things? Point and say.
**C:** letter • post office
**B:** Find the vehicle. What is it?
**A:** It's a truck.

**Track 39:**
**A:** In town, we shop for shoes.
**B:** Can you find these things? Point and say.
**C:** sandals • shoe store
**B:** Find the vehicle. What is it?
**A:** It's a taxi.

**Track 40:**
**A:** In town, we borrow books.
**B:** Can you find these things? Point and say.
**C:** purse • cell phone
**B:** Find the vehicle. What is it?
**A:** It's an airplane.

**Track 41:**
**A:** In town, we go to a movie.
**B:** Can you find these things? Point and say.
**C:** popcorn • mountain
**B:** Find the vehicle. What is it?
**A:** It's a helicopter.

**Track 42:**
**A:** In town, we visit a museum.
**B:** Can you find these things? Point and say.
**C:** mouse
**B:** Find the vehicle. What is it?
**A:** It's a ship.

**Track 43:**
**A:** In town, we eat at a restaurant.
**B:** Can you find these things? Point and say.
**C:** pizza • spaghetti
**B:** Find the vehicle. What is it?
**A:** It's a fire engine.

**Track 50:**
**A:** At the beach, we put on sun block.
**B:** Can you find these things? Point and say.
**C:** sunglasses • island • sea
**B:** Look at the island. What's it like?
**A:** It's far.

**Track 51:**
**A:** At the beach, we play in the sea.
**B:** Can you find these things? Point and say.
**C:** dolphin • island
**B:** Look at the dolphin. What's it like?
**A:** It's near.

**Track 52:**
**A:** At the beach, we build sand castles.
**B:** Can you find these things? Point and say.
**C:** sand castle • sea
**B:** Look at the shovel. What's it like?
**A:** It's long.

**Track 53:**
**A:** At the beach, we chase crabs.
**B:** Can you find these things? Point and say.
**C:** net • crab • seal
**B:** Look at the net. What's it like?
**A:** It's short.

**Track 54:**
**A:** At the beach, we swim.
**B:** Can you find these things? Point and say.
**C:** beach ball • fish
**B:** Look at the beach ball. What's it like?
**A:** It's light.

**Track 55:**
**A:** At the beach, we go for a boat ride.
**B:** Can you find these things? Point and say.
**C:** whale • octopus • shark
**B:** Look at the anchor. What's it like?
**A:** It's heavy.

**Track 56:**
**A:** At the beach, we find shells.
**B:** Can you find these things? Point and say.
**C:** shells • turtle
**B:** Look at the bucket. What's it like?
**A:** It's full.

**Track 57:**
**A:** At the beach, we have a picnic.
**B:** Can you find these things? Point and say.
**C:** basket • peach
**B:** Look at the picnic basket. What's it like?
**A:** It's empty.

**Track 64:**
**A:** At the zoo, we buy tickets.
**B:** Can you find the animal? Point and say.
**C:** gorilla • snake • zebra
**B:** What time is it?
**A:** It's ten o'clock.

**Track 65:**
**A:** At the zoo, we learn about animals.
**B:** Can you find the animal? Point and say.
**C:** hippo • crocodile
**B:** What time is it?
**A:** It's ten fifteen.

**Track 66:**
**A:** At the zoo, we watch feeding time.
**B:** Can you find the animal? Point and say.
**C:** pelican • penguin
**B:** What time is it?
**A:** It's ten thirty.

**Track 67:**
**A:** At the zoo, we drink juice.
**B:** Can you find the animal? Point and say.
**C:** koala • kangaroo
**B:** What time is it?
**A:** It's ten forty-five.

**Track 68:**
**A:** At the zoo, we pet animals.
**B:** Can you find the animal? Point and say.
**C:** rabbit
**B:** What time is it?
**A:** It's eleven o'clock.

**Track 69:**
**A:** At the zoo, we meet our friends.
**B:** Can you find the animal? Point and say.
**C:** elephant
**B:** What time is it?
**A:** It's eleven thirty.

**Track 70:**
**A:** At the zoo, we eat lunch.
**B:** Can you find the animal? Point and say.
**C:** bear • tiger • lion
**B:** What time is it?
**A:** It's twelve o'clock.

**Track 71:**
**A:** At the zoo, we take pictures.
**B:** Can you find the animal? Point and say.
**C:** giraffe • monkey
**B:** What time is it?
**A:** It's one o'clock.

**Track 78:**
**A:** On the farm, we milk cows.
**B:** Can you find these things? Point and say.
**C:** cow
**B:** Who is with Joy?
**A:** Her father.

**Track 79:**
**A:** On the farm, we ride horses.
**B:** Can you find these things? Point and say.
**C:** horse • rainbow
**B:** Who is with Joy?
**A:** Her mother.

**Track 80:**
**A:** On the farm, we feed pigs.
**B:** Can you find these things? Point and say.
**C:** pig • apple
**B:** Who is with Joy?
**A:** Her brother.

**Track 81:**
**A:** On the farm, we play with puppies.
**B:** Can you find these things? Point and say.
**C:** stick • tractor
**B:** Who is with Joy?
**A:** Her sister.

**Track 82:**
**A:** On the farm, we collect eggs.
**B:** Can you find these things? Point and say.
**C:** hen • basket
**B:** Who is with Joy?
**A:** Her uncle.

**Track 83:**
**A:** On the farm, we pick berries.
**B:** Can you find these things? Point and say.
**C:** sheep • berries
**B:** Who is with Joy?
**A:** Her aunt.

**Track 84:**
**A:** On the farm, we make pies.
**B:** Can you find these things? Point and say.
**C:** berries
**B:** Who is with Joy?
**A:** Her grandmother.

**Track 85:**
**A:** On the farm, we have a great time!
**B:** Can you find these things? Point and say.
**C:** duck • pie
**B:** Who is with Joy?
**A:** Her grandfather.

# Model and Extended Readings

You may find it helpful to have a detailed example of how to teach a reading session using a **Potato Pals** reader. The reading below gives an example of one way to introduce "At the Store." You can use this as a model for the other books.

After the example, we provide you with extended readings for each reader. If your students already have some English language ability, you may be able to use these extended readings very effectively.

## "At the Store" model reading:

**Teacher/Parent:** *Now let's read "At the Store." It's about Dean going shopping with his mother and baby sister, Dee. Do you like shopping? What do you like to buy? Let's look at the first page.*

*We get a cart.*

**Students:** *We get a cart.*

**T/P:** *Good. What's that?* (Point to the bicycle.)

**S:** *Bicycle.*

**T/P:** *Yes, it's a bicycle. Great! And what's that?* (Point to one of the cars.)

**S:** *It's a car.*

**T/P:** *That's right. And what's that?* (Point to the baby.)

**S:** *It's a baby.*

**T/P:** *That's right. It's Dee. Good job! Now can you tell me what the baby is doing?* (Point to Dee.)

**S:** *Pulling.*

**T/P:** *Yes! Good. She's pulling the cart.*

**S:** *She's pulling the cart.*

**T/P:** *Let's say it again:* **We get a cart.**

**S:** *We get a cart.*

**T/P:** *Wonderful!* (Turn page.) **At the store, we go inside.**

**S:** *At the store, we go inside.*

**T/P:** *Good. What are those?*

**S:** *Onions.*

**T/P:** *Yes, they are onions. And what are those?*

**S:** *They're carrots.*

**T/P:** *That's right! Can you see Dee? What's she doing?*

**S:** *She's pushing.*

**T/P:** *Yes, she's pushing the cart! What's that?* (Point to Memoricon for "We get a cart.")

**S:** *We get a cart.*

**T/P:** *Good!* (Point to sentence on page again.) *We get a cart. We go inside. Can you say "At the store, we get a cart. We go inside"?*

**S:** *At the store, we get a cart. We go inside.* (Turn the page.)

# Extended Readings

## Book A: At the Store

1. Dean, his mother, and his little sister Dee are going shopping. They need a cart. "The carts are over there! Let's use this one. Pull! Let's go!"

2. Dean and Dee are pushing the cart through the doors. Not too fast now! Be careful not to bump into anyone. What lovely vegetables. I can see onions, carrots, and cabbages. Do you like vegetables?

3. Mmm! Where are the bananas? Dee can see them. She's pointing to them over there. Oh, my! What's happening? The man bumped into the oranges! They are falling on the ground. What other fruit can you see? There are apples, grapes, and pineapples. Which do you like best?

4. Wow! The cart is getting really full. What have they put in it? Bread, orange juice, cherries, and diapers for Dee. Don't break the eggs now! What's that, Dean? Honey? Dean has a sweet tooth. How about you?

5. "We have been waiting a long time in line. We are next! Can you see Daisy's mother? She's after us in line. Oh, Dee! You should not throw things. Watch out, Dean! The tomato is going to hit you on the head!"

6. Now it's their turn to pay. How much is it? Dean's mom has taken out her purse to pay the clerk. Oh, no! She has dropped a coin. Dee is going to catch it. Nice catch, Dee!

7. "Let's put everything in bags now. There's the cheese . . . . Don't forget the chocolate, Mom!" Dean is juggling some eggs. Dee thinks he's funny. She is clapping for him. They will break if you drop them, Dean!

8. All done now. It's time to go home. What's that noise? It's a motorcycle on the road. Dean and Dee are helping by carrying the heavy watermelon and melon. There isn't room for everything in the trunk, so they have put some bags on the roof. Isn't that clever?

## Book B: On a Camping Trip

1. Whee! Daisy and her family love to ride through the countryside in their open car. It feels great having the wind blowing in your hair. It's early in the morning. The sun is rising.

2. Which way are they going to go? What does that sign say? Left for the waterfall or right for the mountain? Dad's got so much stuff to carry. He's moving very slowly. Is that the tent in that big box?

3. "I don't think that's right, Dad! It doesn't look like the picture in the instructions at all." Even the birds think that something's wrong! Maybe Dad should start again.

4. Daisy and the twins have caught some lovely fish. Well done, girls. Dad has caught an old boot! Poor old Dad is having a really unlucky day so far. He can't barbecue that old boot and he can't wear it, either!

5. Now it's evening and the sun is going down behind the mountain. It's time to eat! Dad loves to barbecue. What's on the menu, Dad? Steak, sausages, hot dogs, chicken, fish, salad, and very big corn!

6. After dinner, they sit around the fire and sing all of their favorite songs. There's a squirrel in the tree eating his dinner. It's an acorn. "Dad . . . that guitar is much too small for you!"

7. Daisy and her family are ready to go to bed . . . but wait! Look at that shooting star! Make a wish everyone! Even the fox and the wise old owl are making a wish.

8. The end of a happy day. Mom and Dad are checking on the kids before they go to sleep. Keep warm in those sleeping bags! Good night, everyone!

## Book C: In Town

1. Chip is in town at the candy store. What a lot of candy he has! There's Nina. She loves candy, too. Look at the jars of candy on the shelves. What shapes can you see? Wow! A train full of lollipops. Yum!

2. We're at the barber shop now. Chip and Buddy are getting haircuts, but when Buddy takes his cap off . . . he only has one hair! His barber isn't sure what to do! What's that noise? Oh! It's the siren of an ambulance.

3. Chip is at the post office with Daisy. They are mailing letters. Who did you write a letter to, Chip? Your friend? How about Daisy? Buddy's mom is carrying a package and the mail carrier has a sack of mail. Look at that bright red mail truck!

4. Chip needs some new shoes. He likes the yellow ones with all the stars on them, but Dad isn't so sure. He thinks they are too bright. Can you see the taxi going by outside?

5. Chip and Dean like to go to the library. Chip likes books about animals. That's a deer, isn't it? Dean likes airplanes. You have to be very quiet when you're in a library. No talking or running. Oh, no! Mom's cell phone is ringing! "Shhhhhh!"

6. That looks like a very exciting movie. Chip is really enjoying it. In fact, he's so excited that he's spilling his popcorn. Hurray! The helicopter is rescuing the potatoes who got lost in the mountains.

7. In the museum you can see a lot of old and beautiful things. Buddy and Dean are looking at a picture of a potato pirate from long ago. He is on his sailing ship. There is an even older statue of a potato emperor. Hello, little mouse!

8. Everyone's really hungry after that busy day in town. All of the Pals are at a restaurant. Can you see the different things that they are eating? What do you like best? There goes a fire engine on its way to put out a fire. Chip is very excited. Be careful, Chip! Your orange juice is spilling!

## Book D: At the Beach

1. When you go out in the hot sun, you should always put on sun block. Nina's dad is putting sun block on Nina's mom. Nina's mom is putting sun block on Nina. That island is very far away. Is that a coconut tree?

2. That's amazing, Nina! You can surf! Ride that wave! Joy is in a kayak and Buddy is sailing in his little boat. Hey! That's a dolphin. It's really near to Nina. Is it saying hello?

3. Nina and Chip have built a lovely sand castle. They decorated it with some beautiful pink and purple sea shells. Daisy's kite is flying in the wind. Chip has a nice red bucket and a very long shovel.

4. Those crabs are very fast and they don't want to be caught! Buddy's net is too short to catch the crab on the big rock. He can't reach that high. The seal is wondering what's happening! He's enjoying the sun.

5. Potatoes are all very good swimmers. Daisy can even swim underwater when she has her goggles on. How many fish can you see, Daisy? Chip is throwing the beach ball to Joy. It's very light.

6. Whales! They're very big, aren't they? Nina is very happy to see them. The sailor on the boat is trying to lift up the heavy anchor. Pull! But the octopus is making it even heavier. That shark looks like it's smiling! Do you like the shrimp design on the sail?

7. What a beautiful light blue shell you found, Nina! Are you going to give it to Dean? No? Why not? Oh, I see. His bucket is too full. Can you see the turtle on the rock over there? What about the red and white lighthouse?

8. "I'm hungry!" "Me, too!" It's nice eating outside in the fresh air. Who's there? Mom and Dad, with Nina, Daisy, Buddy, and Chip. What a lot of delicious things to eat. Doughnuts, sandwiches, chicken, and peaches. Yum!

## Book E: At the Zoo

1. "Three tickets, please! Thank you very much. I like your posters, Mr. Zookeeper. Can we really see gorillas and snakes here? I can't wait! Come on! Let's go!"

2. Look at the man talking about the animals. He is pointing to Africa where many of these animals live: crocodiles, hippos, ostriches, and flamingos. The hippo is yawning. Is it sleepy?

3. How many fish can a pelican eat with that big beak? A whole bucket? "Hey, can we have some, too, please?" say the penguins, the seal, and the walrus. Maybe they will eat next!

4. Buddy and his brother Buzz are thirsty. They will buy a drink at the stand. Mmmm! That's good. They can buy toys there, too. Those kangaroos and koalas are so cute.

5. That rabbit is cute, too! Its fur is very soft. Look at the goat's long beard and the sheep's thick wool. There are ducks, too. Hear them say "Quack, quack!"

6. "Hi, Chip! How are you?" "Fine, thank you! How are you?" Buddy and Chip are so pleased to meet that they don't notice the elephant giving its baby a shower. Splash!

7. After watching all those animals being fed, it's the Potato Pals' turn. Everyone is enjoying themselves and there are plenty of sandwiches. The bear, tiger, and lion already had their lunch.

8. "Let's take a picture so we'll always remember this great day. Okay, everyone! Stand still. Smile! Cheese! Hey! What is that monkey doing?" The monkey is trying to take Buddy's dad's hat!

## Book F: On the Farm

1. It's early in the morning. The first job today is to milk the cow. She makes a lot of delicious milk for us. Joy's dad is very good at milking her. Joy wants to try, too.

2. The most exciting thing to do on the farm is to ride horses. Joy and her mother sometimes ride far from the house. Joy's mom rides a horse that is bigger than Joy's pony. Look at the beautiful rainbow in the sky!

3. Joy is feeding the pigs with her brother, Jake. The hungry pigs eat buckets and buckets of apples and carrots every day. They eat so fast and make such a noise. Slow down, pigs!

4. Joy and her sister Jenny love the puppies. They're so sweet. Joy can throw the stick a long way and the puppies try to catch it. Which puppy is going to get it? Here comes the tractor. Vroom, vroom!

5. One, two, three, four hens are sitting on their nests. Joy's uncle takes care of the hens. He collects their eggs every day. Thank you, hens! You are very kind to give us your eggs.

6. Joy and her aunt almost have a full basket of berries now. Just a few more. One, two, three! That's enough now. Oh! They've dropped one on the ground and the mouse is going to take it! Lucky mouse!

7. The kitchen is the busiest place on the farm when Grandma starts cooking pies. It can get pretty messy and the cat usually gets some, too! How many pies are they making? There is one in the oven and one on the table. Is Joy making another one from those delicious berries?

8. All the family are sitting down together and about to eat those yummy-looking pies! Joy is cutting and serving the first pie. Grandpa is bringing the second one to the table. What a wonderful day on the farm! Good-bye, everyone! Enjoy the pies!

## Instructions and Answer Keys for Activity Book and Workbook

## Teachers and Parents, try to do the following:

- Use the Activity Book and Workbook to practice the Story Sentences, Focus Words, and Topic Words from Book Set 2.

- Try to pace your students' progress so that they are practicing the language from the readers at the same time as they are using the Activity Book and/or Workbook.

- Encourage students to say the words as they do the activities in the practice books.

- When all students have finished a page, it is useful to review quickly the work that they did. Repeat the words and phrases.

- Play the song from that reader in the background while your students do the activities.

### Activity Book

**Page 2**
Students match the pictures with the pictures of the potatoes and color.

**1.** c  **2.** d  **3.** b  **4.** a

**Page 3**
Students match the silhouettes with the picture cues.

**1.** b  **2.** d  **3.** a  **4.** c

**Page 4**
Students help the Potato Pals do their shopping by connecting the pictures to the correct shopping list.

**Page 5**
Students circle the one that is different and color the pictures.

**1.** b  **2.** c  **3.** b  **4.** a  **5.** b

**Page 6**
Students connect the Potato Pals doing the same actions.

**1.** 2nd picture, c
**2.** 3rd picture, a
**3.** 4th picture, b
**4.** 1st picture, d

**Page 7**
Students finish the drawings and color.

**Page 8**
Students connect the objects that start with the same sound with the letters in the middle. Then they color the pictures.

**b:** bananas, bread, bicycle
**m:** money, milk, melon

**Page 9**
Students circle the differences and color the pictures. Each number has two differences.

**1.** In a, Daisy and one of her sisters are standing by the river and Daisy has caught a fish. In b, the sisters are sitting on a log and Daisy's sister has caught a fish, too.

**2.** In a, there is a hot dog on the plate and a fork on the table. In b, there is a steak on the plate and a spoon on the table.

**3.** In a, the twins are looking at the shooting star and there is a mountain in the background. In b, there are two mountains and the twins' mother stands with them.

**4.** In a, Daisy and her father are sitting on a log singing songs. There is a fishing rod next to the log and Daisy's father does not wear a hat. In b, Daisy's father wears a hat and there is a backpack next to the log.

**Page 10**
Students find their way through the maze, then color.

**Page 11**
Students find the shapes of the objects and color.

**Page 12**
Students find the objects in the picture and color.

**Page 13**
Students trace the objects and color.

**Page 14**
Students match the pictures and color.

**1.** c  **2.** b  **3.** d  **4.** a

**Page 15**
Students connect the objects to the correct box, draw, and color.

**f:** fish, fox, flashlight
**s:** salad, squirrel, star

**Page 16**
Students match the picture cues with the objects, trace and color.

**1.** c  **2.** a  **3.** d  **4.** b

**Page 17**
Students find out what the Potato Pals are doing in town.

**1.** We eat at a restaurant.
**2.** We visit a museum.
**3.** We go to a movie.
**4.** We borrow books.

**Page 18**
Students match the objects.

**1.** b    **2.** e    **3.** a
**4.** c    **5.** f    **6.** d

**Page 19**
Students match the Potato Pals with the places.

**1.** e      **2.** c      **3.** a
**4.** d      **5.** b

**Page 20**
Students trace the objects and color.

**Page 21**
Students connect the objects, trace, and color.

**1.** c    **2.** d    **3.** b    **4.** a

**Page 22**
Students write the letters and connect them with the objects that start with the same sound.

**t:** taxi, truck, train
**p:** purse, pizza, popcorn

**Page 23**
Students connect the pictures with the objects, trace, and color.

**1.** d    **2.** a    **3.** b    **4.** c

**Page 24**
Students connect the picture cues to the Potato Pals in the picture and color.

**Page 25**
Students trace and color the objects, then connect them to the silhouettes.

**1.** c      **2.** e      **3.** d
**4.** b      **5.** a

**Page 26**
Students find the objects and color.

**Page 27**
Students connect the opposites and color.

**1.** d    **2.** a    **3.** c    **4.** b

**Page 28**
Students circle the picture that's different and color.

**1.** d    **2.** a    **3.** b    **4.** c

**Page 29**
Students write **s** and connect the objects that start with that sound.

**s:** sand castle, seal, sea, sandwich, sunglasses, shark

**Page 30**
Students match the picture cues with the Potato Pals.

**1.** c    **2.** a    **3.** d    **4.** b

**Page 31**
Students find the way through the maze.

**Page 32**
Students trace the pictures and color.

**Page 33**
Students connect the animals and color.

**1.** b    **2.** c    **3.** a    **4.** d

**Page 34**
Students trace the clocks and match them with the Potato Pals.

**1.** d    **2.** c    **3.** a    **4.** b

**Page 35**
Students trace and draw the times.

**Page 36**
Students write the letters and circle the objects that start with that sound.

**1.** a, b
**2.** b, c
**3.** a, c
**4.** a, b

**Page 37**
Students match the silhouettes with the Potato Pals and color.

**1.** c    **2.** a    **3.** d    **4.** b

**Page 38**
Students find out what the Potato Pals are doing on the farm.

**1.** we collect eggs.
**2.** we have a great time!
**3.** we make pies.
**4.** we pick berries.

**Page 39**
Students find the animals in the picture and color.

**Page 40**
Students circle the object that is the same.

**1.** b        **3.** c
**2.** b        **4.** c

**Page 41**
Students connect Joy and her family member with the same family member on the right.

**1.** b    **2.** c    **3.** d    **4.** a

**Page 42**
Students connect the family members that are the same and color.

**1.** c    **2.** a    **3.** d    **4.** b

**Page 43**
Students trace the pictures, color, and write the letters.

**Page 44**
Students draw a picture of their favorite animal and color.

**Page 45**
Students draw some Potato Pals in town and then color the picture.

**Page 46**
Students draw some big things and some small things.

# Workbook

### Page 2
Students help Dean and his family go through the maze.

### Page 3
Students look at the picture cues and write the words.

   **1.** get   **2.** wait   **3.** fill   **4.** go

### Page 4
Students do the crossword puzzle.

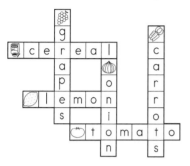

### Page 5
Students write the words and find them.

### Page 6
Students write the words, trace the pictures, and color.

   **1.** pull        **3.** throw
   **2.** push       **4.** catch

### Page 7
Students match the pictures and write the words.

   **1.** b, point   **3.** d, clap
   **2.** c, shake   **4.** a, carry

### Page 8
Students help Dean's mom do her shopping. They write and then match.

      milk, melon, bread, bananas, cookies, cabbage

### Page 9
Students trace the pictures, write the words, and color.

### Page 10
Students look at the pictures and write the words.

   **1.** fishing     **3.** Good night
   **2.** barbecue   **4.** hiking

### Page 11
Students finish the pictures, write the words, and color.

### Page 12
Students write the words and color the pictures.

   **1.** sky        **4.** fire
   **2.** star       **5.** leaves
   **3.** corn      **6.** river

### Page 13
Students connect the pictures and write the words.

   **1.** b   **2.** d   **3.** a   **4.** c

### Page 14
Students connect the opposites.

   **1.** d   **2.** c   **3.** b   **4.** a

### Page 15
Students write the letters, write the words, and color the picture.

   **1.** f          **4.** f
   **2.** t          **5.** s
   **3.** t          **6.** s

### Page 16
Students connect the picture cues with the pictures of Chip in town to finish the sentences.

   **1.** b   **2.** a   **3.** d   **4.** c

### Page 17
Students connect the half picture cues and write the words.

   **1.** c   **2.** d   **3.** a   **4.** b

### Page 18
Students write the words.

   **1.** cell phone   **4.** mouse
   **2.** spaghetti    **5.** sandals
   **3.** purse       **6.** balloon

### Page 19
Students help the Potato Pals to find the places they need to go.

   **1.** b   **2.** a   **3.** d   **4.** c

### Page 20
Students write the words.

   **1.** ambulance   **4.** airplane
   **2.** train        **5.** truck
   **3.** ship         **6.** helicopter

### Page 21
Students find what's missing and write the words.

   **1.** train        **3.** fire engine
   **2.** ambulance   **4.** taxi

### Page 22
Students write the letters and words.

   **1. l**etter       **4. p**opcorn
   **2. l**ibrary     **5. m**useum
   **3. p**izza       **6. m**ouse

### Page 23
Students write the words.

   **1.** play      **3.** put on
   **2.** have     **4.** go

### Page 24
Students connect the half picture clues and write the words.

   **1.** build    **3.** chase
   **2.** find     **4.** swim

### Page 25
Students do the crossword puzzle.

### Page 26
Students find what's missing, draw and color the pictures, then write the words.

   **1.** octopus   **3.** crab
   **2.** shark     **4.** whale

### Page 27
Students trace the objects, color the pictures, and write the words.

### Page 28
Students trace, write the words, and color.

### Page 29
Students write the words.

   **1.** sandwich     **4.** sea
   **2.** sunglasses   **5.** seal
   **3.** sand castle   **6.** shells

**Page 30**
Students write the words and match the picture cues with the close-ups.

**1.** c    **2.** a    **3.** b

**Page 31**
Students choose the words and match the picture cues with the close-ups.

**1.** animals    **4.** lunch
**2.** tickets    **5.** pictures
**3.** friends

**Page 32**
Students write the words.

**1.** zebra    **3.** giraffe
**2.** kangaroo    **4.** monkey

**Page 33**
Students find and circle the words, then color.

| r | a | b | p | e | b | e | a | r | k |
|---|---|---|---|---|---|---|---|---|---|
| h | i | p | p | o | v | h | r | n | o |
| n | i | s | m | y | k | o | a | l | a |
| r | b | c | t | v | l | j | v | m | t |
| g | o | r | i | l | l | a | o | p | e |
| l | i | o | n | o | s | n | a | k | e |
| r | j | p | i | r | a | b | b | i | t |
| l | e | e | l | e | p | h | a | n | t |

**Page 34**
Students draw the hands, connect the clocks, and write the times.

**1.** d, 10:00    **3.** a, 12:00
**2.** c, 11:00    **4.** b, 1:00

**Page 35**
Students circle the times that are the same.

**1.** a    **2.** c    **3.** c    **4.** b    **5.** b

**Page 36**
Students write the words and letters and then connect them to the objects that start with those sounds.

**t:** ticket, tiger
**c:** camera, crocodile
**p:** pelican, penguin

**Page 37**
Students connect the pictures with the picture cues, write the words, and color.

**1.** b, ride
**2.** c, pick
**3.** a, milk

**Page 38**
Students write the missing sentences.

**1.** We make pies.
**2.** We collect eggs.
**3.** We feed pigs.

**Page 39**
Students match the animals and then draw.

**1.** c    **2.** a    **3.** d    **4.** b

**Page 40**
Students find the pattern in the grid and write the words.

**1.** rainbow    **3.** stick
**2.** tractor    **4.** apple

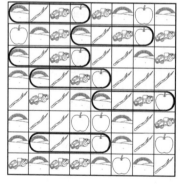

**Page 41**
Students write the words and color the picture.

**1.** father    **3.** mother
**2.** sister    **4.** brother

**Page 42**
Students write the words and color the picture.

**1.** grandmother
**2.** grandfather
**3.** uncle
**4.** aunt

**Page 43**
Students write the letters, draw the words, and color.

**1.** apple    **3.** duck
**2.** cow    **4.** berries

**Page 44**
Students draw store items in the cart and color. Then they can write one or more of the items.

**Page 45**
Students draw objects in the spaces and color.

**Page 46**
Students draw a potato family trip and color. Then they write what the potatoes are doing (example: "The potatoes are hiking.")

# Potato Awards

**Potato Pals**

Congratulations! You can say all of the sentences in

" _____."

*Well done!*

**Potato Pals**

This certifies that

_____

is a super **Potato Pals** singer!

**Potato Pals**

This certifies that

_____'s

homework is terrific. Excellent work!

# Picture Card List

1 At the store, we get a cart.
2 At the store, we go inside.
3 At the store, we look for things.
4 At the store, we fill the cart.
5 At the store, we wait in line.
6 At the store, we pay.
7 At the store, we put things in bags.
8 At the store, we load the car.

| | | | |
|---|---|---|---|
| 9 | bicycle | 19 | cereal |
| 10 | cart | 20 | tomato |
| 11 | onion | 21 | cookies |
| 12 | carrots | 22 | melon |
| 13 | cabbage | 23 | money |
| 14 | bananas | 24 | cheese |
| 15 | orange | 25 | chocolate |
| 16 | grapes | 26 | lemon |
| 17 | bread | 27 | watermelon |
| 18 | milk | 28 | motorcycle |

| | | | |
|---|---|---|---|
| 29 | pull | 33 | throw |
| 30 | push | 34 | catch |
| 31 | point | 35 | clap |
| 32 | shake | 36 | carry |

37 On a camping trip, we ride in the car.
38 On a camping trip, we go hiking.
39 On a camping trip, we put up our tent.
40 On a camping trip, we go fishing.
41 On a camping trip, we have a barbecue.
42 On a camping trip, we sing songs.
43 On a camping trip, we count the stars.
44 On a camping trip, we say "Good night!"

| | | | |
|---|---|---|---|
| 45 | leaves | 55 | corn |
| 46 | mountain | 56 | hot dog |
| 47 | backpack | 57 | guitar |
| 48 | turtle | 58 | squirrel |
| 49 | tent | 59 | fire |
| 50 | fish | 60 | owl |
| 51 | river | 61 | fox |
| 52 | fishing rod | 62 | star |
| 53 | salad | 63 | flashlight |
| 54 | chicken | 64 | sky |

| | | | |
|---|---|---|---|
| 65 | fast | 69 | big |
| 66 | slow | 70 | small |
| 67 | new | 71 | bright |
| 68 | old | 72 | dark |

73 In town, we buy candy.
74 In town, we get haircuts.
75 In town, we mail letters.
76 In town, we shop for shoes.
77 In town, we borrow books.
78 In town, we go to a movie.
79 In town, we visit a museum.
80 In town, we eat at a restaurant.

| | | | |
|---|---|---|---|
| 81 | candy | 90 | cell phone |
| 82 | balloon | 91 | library |
| 83 | candy store | 92 | popcorn |
| 84 | barber shop | 93 | movie theater |
| 85 | letter | 94 | mouse |
| 86 | post office | 95 | museum |
| 87 | sandals | 96 | pizza |
| 88 | shoe store | 97 | spaghetti |
| 89 | purse | 98 | restaurant |

| | | | |
|---|---|---|---|
| 99 | train | 103 | airplane |
| 100 | ambulance | 104 | helicopter |
| 101 | truck | 105 | ship |
| 102 | taxi | 106 | fire engine |

107 At the beach, we put on sun block.
108 At the beach, we play in the sea.
109 At the beach, we build sand castles.
110 At the beach, we chase crabs.
111 At the beach, we swim.
112 At the beach, we go for a boat ride.
113 At the beach, we find shells.
114 At the beach, we have a picnic.

| | | | |
|---|---|---|---|
| 115 | sunglasses | 124 | whale |
| 116 | sea | 125 | anchor |
| 117 | island | 126 | octopus |
| 118 | dolphin | 127 | shark |
| 119 | sand castle | 128 | shells |
| 120 | crab | 129 | sandwich |
| 121 | net | 130 | peach |
| 122 | seal | 131 | basket |
| 123 | beach ball | | |

| | | | |
|---|---|---|---|
| 132 | far | 136 | light |
| 133 | near | 137 | heavy |
| 134 | long | 138 | full |
| 135 | short | 139 | empty |

140 At the zoo, we buy tickets.
141 At the zoo, we learn about animals.
142 At the zoo, we watch feeding time.
143 At the zoo, we drink juice.
144 At the zoo, we pet animals.
145 At the zoo, we meet our friends.
146 At the zoo, we eat lunch.
147 At the zoo, we take pictures.

| | | | |
|---|---|---|---|
| 148 | ticket | 157 | kangaroo |
| 149 | gorilla | 158 | rabbit |
| 150 | snake | 159 | elephant |
| 151 | zebra | 160 | bear |
| 152 | hippo | 161 | tiger |
| 153 | crocodile | 162 | lion |
| 154 | pelican | 163 | camera |
| 155 | penguin | 164 | giraffe |
| 156 | koala | 165 | monkey |

| | |
|---|---|
| 166 | 10:00 (ten o'clock) |
| 167 | 10:15 (ten fifteen) |
| 168 | 10:30 (ten thirty) |
| 169 | 10:45 (ten forty-five) |
| 170 | 11:00 (eleven o'clock) |
| 171 | 11:30 (eleven thirty) |
| 172 | 12:00 (twelve o'clock) |
| 173 | 1:00 (one o'clock) |

174 On the farm, we milk cows.
175 On the farm, we ride horses.
176 On the farm, we feed pigs.
177 On the farm, we play with puppies.
178 On the farm, we collect eggs.
179 On the farm, we pick berries.
180 On the farm, we make pies.
181 On the farm, we have a great time!

| | | | |
|---|---|---|---|
| 182 | cow | 188 | tractor |
| 183 | horse | 189 | hen |
| 184 | rainbow | 190 | sheep |
| 185 | pig | 191 | berries |
| 186 | apple | 192 | duck |
| 187 | stick | | |

| | | | |
|---|---|---|---|
| 193 | father | 197 | uncle |
| 194 | mother | 198 | aunt |
| 195 | brother | 199 | grandmother |
| 196 | sister | 200 | grandfather |

# Index